THE WORD ARK

a pocket book of

ANIMAL POEMS

First published in 2020 by
The Dedalus Press
13 Moyclare Road
Baldoyle
Dublin D13 K1C2
Ireland

www.**dedaluspress**.com

ISBN 978 1 910251 75 1 (paperback)
ISBN 978 1 910251 76 8 (hardback)

Typesetting & Design: Pat Boran
Illustrations: Gaetano Tranchino

The Dedalus Press receives financial assistance from
The Arts Council / An Chomhairle Ealaíon.

THE WORD ARK

a pocket book of

ANIMAL POEMS

Edited by
PAT BORAN

With illustrations by
Gaetano Tranchino

DEDALUS PRESS

Until one has loved an animal,
a part of one's soul remains unawakened.
—Anatole France

Contents

INTRODUCTION

This pocket book of animal poems grew, almost organically, out of a very modest impulse.

Towards the end of 2019 I had the idea of gathering a dozen or so of the animal poems I'd written over recent years, to publish them (perhaps with illustrations) as a kind of New Year's mini-project, a way of looking back and, at the same time, of clearing new ground for myself. As I started to play around with it, I found myself dipping back into the 150 or so titles I'd produced for the Dedalus Press, and was fascinated to discover a real wealth of animals poems therein.

As so often happens, my original idea for a small, private publication began to morph and evolve into something considerably more ambitious. Instead of a handful of poems, before long I had a large and growing list of contenders, all jostling and braying for admission to what would soon become *The Word Ark*.

As I continued to gather and sequence into late January and early February, the Covid-19 crisis was already spreading inexorably across the globe (not least in Italy, which certainly 'brought it home' to our Irish-Italian family unit here in north Dublin). Suddenly so many of our plans and ambitions seemed trivial if not utterly irrelevant.

With the passing weeks, and the inevitable lockdowns now in place (a radius of 2km here in Ireland, of just 200m for my Sicilian in-laws), all of us began to feel a growing sense of powerlessness, the novelty of video-conferencing falling far short of actual, flesh-and-blood encounters. And yet, rather than shelve or defer my 'pet project', I began to feel certain that a publication of this sort was very much a fitting response to these strange times – an invitation to look more intently at the world beyond ourselves, an external balance to our inner turmoil. I was delighted, of course, that my fellow poets were in enthusiastic accord.

Who knows, a more comprehensive anthology might well be issued at another time, perhaps one that looks even farther afield than the poets associated with this one small publishing house. But, as is often the case with the creative impulse, it seemed important in this instance to act quickly and decisively, to make something timely, portable and simple, something that students of the natural world might wish to carry with them on future expeditions, whether into the alarmingly diminishing wilds or just down to the deckchair at the cool end of the garden.

It turns out that, even as we grieve and mourn – and even live in dread of what may come next – we can also love and laud and celebrate. In truth, it may be more important than ever that we do so, certainly for the creatures with whom we share this planet, but also for our own mental health and psychic well-being. For out of the kind of attention a poem requires – first of its writer, and then of its readers – a more sensitive and considerate way of being together in the world might yet emerge

I am particularly grateful to my father-in-law Gaetano Tranchino *(www.gaetanotranchino.com)* who, in a spirit of solidarity and fun, contributed the charming illustrations that grace and lift the pages of this little book.

— PB

ANIMAL ENCOUNTERS

It was a small kitchen and hot,
no proper work surfaces, no ventilation –
but the ants didn't mind. Evenings they came

unspooling through the pantry, unwinding
over cupboards, probing for any crumb.
And one night I came home late, drunk,

to find the place infested, a black flood
of ant armies travelling like neurons
straight to my instincts, direct to murderous rage.

I went at them as if they
had declared war on my children.
I don't want to tell you the things I did.

All week I had been thinking
about animal encounters –
the messages creatures bring.

For so long I had wanted
to read augury,
to grow fluent in omen.

So what could it portend, a woman
in her midnight kitchen –
a crazed exterminator

bashing at ants with her broom,
pouring boiling water,
scooping her dark harvest into a pail?

GRACE WELLS

BADGER

I've never seen you alive:
You're from stories, riverbank tales
of a gentleman in a dinner jacket,
the solid citizen who prevails.

A mystery like your name:
Are you badged head or corn-hoarder,
or grey man, the Irish *broc*,
a fugitive living on the border?

Holing up in a dug-out,
solitary or thick as thieves,
covering miles in the night
to reach a safe house, eaves-
dropping on your foes without a sound,
giving no quarter when you clamp down.

CATHERINE ANN CULLEN

ODE TO A BADGER

us in a dirt mirror a lurching likeness
bearded Hyde keeps to himself

comes out late at night
hectic digger of sullen dreams

elder uncle
horatian headache

secret carnivore
has claws   can kill

gnaws on bark
scared his face white

his laugh he lost
in his throat

little gorilla
with soot-saddened eyes

feasts on roots
and moonlight

there was always one
around the house

white-faced
black-striped

why you so moody
sniffed the sunrise

and swallowed the sun
badger   baritone of loneliness

hoarse barker
tired of anything bright

angry dog
gorged on the whimsical

rabbit big weasel
coughing grumpster

querulous mole
big brother to the moon

nostalgic for blood and fever
shakes his head at ignited cats

once he heard the lark
now there is nothing

if you meet a dead relative
in one of these setts

sniff and move on
no point in mourning

king of charred hearts
and proud of it

crooked smiling minister
of the unrequited

sorry bear
closing your eyes to colour

clandestine neighbour
not unlike ourselves

when in fear
secretes repugnant scents

characteristic of the weasel family
brother to the skunk

PAUL PERRY

THE BAT

Church doors wide open,
the bat came flying in
that October evening,

dark wings splayed,
swooped over the congregation
in packed pews,

across the silent altar,
stirring the air above
the celebrant,

drew a ripple from children
gathered for Communion,
levitated for their eyes.

Flew high as the rafters,
creature of night skies,
tiny claws quivered past

solemn readings from Isaiah,
the Gospel of St Mark?
Chose this occasion

to run amok,
to turn the heads of girls
in best dresses,

small boys in long pants,
break all the rules,
eerily, to dance?

CATHERINE PHIL MacCARTHY

THE BEAR

Pigmentation on cave walls,
a man thinking
to capture an animal,
or maybe to capture
an animal's way of thinking.

And in my parish a man
who could cajole
a bull, another who'd whisper
obedience to even
the most high-spirited horse.

Neither man would tell
his gift. I began to credit
the state of animal
integrity or natured separateness
could be waltzed across.

Except that this bear, he
of the delirious smile
and the murk-coloured fur,
was nobody's dancing companion.
He'd draw his own plans

up out of the ground,
where something had made
the mistake of moving,
or pluck the air down,
a sumptuous banner of smells

invisibly streaming,
and bundle it in wads about him.

What odds a berry bush
evading his juggle,
a salmon his slap, a shellfish

adrift in the sand
his lock-picking hook?
Or, if I was safe in bed, dreaming
myself a bear, this
hand become a bear's grip?

PATRICK DEELEY

OLD BEAR

on the freeway
her coat dusty and threadbare
like an old sofa

she has come inland
to search for the bees
of the horizon

EVA BOURKE

THE JANUARY BEE

who comes to the winter-flowering shrub,
grief in his empty pouches, who sups
alone in the stilled garden this dusk:

I would have missed him only I stopped
mid-argument to watch the moonrise
over the wet roofs of the suburb

and caught him at work deep in the musk,
shaking the bells of the scarce blossoms,
tolling our angers, ringing in peace.

PAULA MEEHAN

SWARM

Search for them in the canopy,
among meadow grasses,

you won't spot them;
the thousands of bees

that unzip the air,
follow the day's weft,

that rip the silence like cloth,
tug the tiny hairs on skin

with their ghost music –
bees long dead, bees soon to die,

as the ladder of evolution
reaches its vanishing point.

They hide here
among birdsfoot trefoil,

purple vetch, self-heal,
among hemlock and nightshade

and they wait,
these phantom bees,

between the dusty pines
with those who have

nothing to fear;
the numberless dead.

JESSICA TRAYNOR

KEEPER OF THE BEES

Father captured wild bees –
teeming brown beards that hung
from tree branches. Carried them
back to hives hidden in the orchard's
rough grass, where the tree dangled
shiny red apples, sour on the tongue.

The bees foraged and hummed in fields
clotted with clover, discordant,
when father leaned over their hives,
my brother beside him, lifting
square bullions up to the sun,
head haloed with bees – the chosen one.

MARIE COVENEY

BEETLE

Little beetle,
    spinning on your back
        like a mad clock,

with a twig
    I flip you over
        and set you off

to work,
    to work you go
        in the family plot.

PAT BORAN

BLACKBIRD

Our blackbird has haunted us
with his summer of song.
And now we cannot imagine him gone
with his wake-up call and long serenade,
constant since we turned back
the clock in April.

In the green lustre
of the tree outside the kitchen
his chatter was like a monologue
of reminiscence. His song of songs
we heard, often before daybreak
more often as our evening entertainment.

Once there were two of them,
with their call and answer: the Peeping Tom
well hidden in the bushes,
the worm-gatherer out front, showing courage.

GERARD SMYTH

BLACKBIRD

for Ciairín, three months pregnant

The scissoring blades had come so close
That I almost sliced the nest and its three
Speckled blue eggs, suddenly and brutally
Exposed, balanced, on a few new shoots
Of the hedge I was cutting. And I thought
She would never return, that the nest
And eggs would shrivel away into a sad
Might have been. But less than an hour
Saw her brown tail again cocked over the nest,
Her yellow beak and accusing eye willing me
Not to betray her again, willing the wind
Not to capsize her world, willing the blades
To hold off awhile. And now a gale has come
And gone, and she is still sitting on the eggs,
And I am holding my breath day after day,
Willing her just a few more weeks of grace.

PADDY BUSHE

'BLACKBIRD ON A POLE'

Blackbird on a pole
watching sanderlings charge past –
air traffic control.

PAT BORAN

BUDGERIGAR

The bay window's net curtains are what we notice first,
their faded, sand-yellow look suggesting a tide
has gone out. Then the tendrils of scrubland grass – as near
to your native habitat as we can get – climbing
the white grid of your cage. Nature programmes on TV
you will answer with a chirrup, or the robin
that comes with morning to the sill, a cross-fertilisation
trying to happen, a tantalising trade-off in song.
But rock music is your favourite, its rhythms 'stomping'
your twig feet, its screech excoriating the world
through your open throat. You don't grow to resemble us,
to appear grateful or to regret. We seem nothing
you could cherish or be improved by, or wish
to cuddle up to in your doubtful role as family pet. Are we
cold-hearted, caging you? Ah, there's a place
we have no wish to go; you occupy one small compartment
in our busy heads that – if it occurs to us – we evade
by means of the make-believe beach beyond
the curtains, the wilderness down-sized to a potted plant.

PATRICK DEELEY

'UP THEY SOAR ...'

Up they soar, the planet's butterflies,
pigments from the warm body of the earth,
cinnabar, ochre, phosphor yellow, gold
a swarm of basic elements aloft.

Is this flickering of wings only a shoal
of light particles, a quirk of perception?
Is it the dreamed summer hour of my childhood
shattered as by lightning lost in time?

No, this is the angel of light, who can paint
himself as dark mnemosyne Apollo,
as copper, hawkmoth, swallowtail.

I see them with my blurred understanding
as feathers in the coverlet of haze
in Brajcino Valley's noon-hot air.

INGER CHRISTENSEN (1935 – 2009)
Opening sonnet of the sonnet cycle 'Butterfly Valley'.
Translated from the Danish by Susanna Nied.

BUTTERFLIES

One afternoon you read me the fourth storey,
names of rooms long unoccupied. Room
after room of faded wallpaper, folding screens
and empty grates. Things stored for generations,
amassed then simply set aside; a hatbox held

a wedding bouquet long dried since its hand-
written note, 1875. Among the layers of Victoriana:
a collection of birds' eggs, binocular cases
and fencing masks. A yellowed Ordinance Survey of Louth
fell from old prints. All seemed new to you, as floorboards
gave off their familiar smell. By the locked room, I found
wings of butterflies disembodied in dust, Small Tortoiseshells
and Red Admirals like petals preserved from some previous
summer, placed in a notebook that may outlast us.

JOSEPH WOODS

WHAT?

I am up close to the radio,
listening late and at low volume
to the World Service
when the house shudders.
My brother is tumbling purposefully
down the stairs.
Eighteen stones of spluttering indignation
in a tiny red underpants,
bearing a message from his wife:
'Would you ever go to bed,
you're keeping the canary awake ...'

GERRY MURPHY

STRANGE FAMILIAR

Not god nor devil brought you.
I neither chose nor own you,
but am bound to you by blood and wonder.

You were the dark shape at my ankles,
weaving between my feet,
one minute clawing the air, all arch and hiss,
the next a soft curl against my breast.

Time was, they might have burnt both of us:
me muttering snatches of rhyme,
you with your constant self-commentary,
your animal companions, your night terrors.

Now you look crooked at me,
your father's fire flickering your nostrils,
and I understand that though he and I
made ourselves whole together,
you made no such contract.

We're caught in that tit for tat:
I too was the spit and image of my father,
a strange familiar to my mother
whose eyes for me were all nonplus and puzzle.

My apron-string kitten,
it seems I turned once in a circle
and found you shapeshifted
to this long-limbed branch-leaper,
walking on air solid as earth,
blending fire and water,
always in your element.

I turn again and catch you
looking out of your Moorish grandmother's almond eyes,
eyes cool and clear as hieroglyphs of eyes.

Your skin, opaque as moonlight,
betrays something of your astral travels.

You are making yourself visible
without a spirit guide,
contained enough to conjure
your own familiar.

CATHERINE ANN CULLEN

LETTING THE CAT OUT OF THE BAG

When my father stole
into the scullery

having faltered over fields
from the flooded quarry,

which naturally we were warned
against and was bottomless,

he announced he'd never
carry out an act like it again:

gathering the kittens
with their mother

and weighting the whole shebang
into a loose-stitched sack.

All the more strange,
even alarming,

when within a week
the mother arrived back

to sit on the windowsill
and observe for some years

my father's uneasy comings and goings.

JOSEPH WOODS

ENCOUNTER

The car crested a gradual rise and down
the long slope of its lea we saw a female
caribou, her whole bearing a checkmate.
As we coasted the decline, she held, broadside,
her panel of torso and haunch like the bulk
of drawing room furniture, its skillful finish of long
tapering legs making a delightful grace
to set the piece at a daringly high centre
of gravity. Her imperious neck; the open skance
of her ears; and her coat that was a hybrid
of season: summer-brown cape; winter-smoke
belly, throat, face; dark swatches from eye
to black nose. That close. Then she turned,
ran. We followed. She showed herself deer fitting
a wasteland: not one for bounding and leaping,
but animal to cover distance with her camel-like
stride, a slung trot, the back unexcited. Her hocks
swooped rhythmically, her fetlocks gave, sprang,
as shovels of hooves slapped the road's surface.

What happened next is not original, but
it doesn't lose in the telling: a story of mutual
gaze, two animals looking across the flatland
of their curiosity. The caribou slewed into the bush.
I stopped the car and got out. She'd already
halted in a shallow arena, waited for me
in a clearing of lichen and shale. To meet her,
I waded slowly through a furze of thigh-high
trees. We were not equal: I had history
to contend her with; she, antlerless, possibly
a mere year old, had only herself and trust
in the magic of her body to spirit her
from danger. Of course I wanted to touch her;
of course I knew she'd never let me; but I walked
on, singing, like a low desperate unconvincing
siren: *Pretty girl, baby, don't be afraid.*
She stared. What she made of me is wild surmise.
What I made of her is churned with ambivalence.
Still, we looked and that looking was equal.

You know what happened next. I crossed
the electric boundary that she'd set me
and she quit. Not rapidly; pensively; a creature
mindful of the deep strangenesses of the world.
Her hesitation gave me hope. I followed,
quietly, to the top of the rise where the Barrens
stretched out with dissolving invariance.
Already she was submerged, her head
poking from a low thicket of spruce.
I was confined to these shallows; could not
pursue further. I bade her well and withdrew.
Then anticipated, dissuaded, shock: *what*
has been called *the famous caribou vacillation …*
that one more look back at what had scared them.

Vacillation to match my own. I was crossing
the shale when I checked. She was swinging
down the slope towards me, big easy strides,
nose lifted and eager. The mystery of forgiveness
is not sweeter. I would have come furred
and graceful as her calf for her to claim me.
It could not be. She had stopped, turned oblique.
To break the tension, that hard measure
of our separateness, I stepped out to her.
She retreated. This time the Barrens
would keep her. Sunlight blanched my body back.
I pawed the shale with my boot. Now
the car, the road's thread, could reel me in.

MARY MONTAGUE

THE ISLAND COW

has the unhurried gait of
a barefooted woman balancing
a gourd of water

on her head. You know she
will never spill as much
as a single drop

of last night's dew from
her back nor tread on
a lark's nest

in the long grass. Her pace
is the pace of the tides,
full moons becalmed

in cloudless skies, scythes
in the stone-walled meadows.
Around the peg

of her tether through the field
of her gravity she moves at
the pace of the seasons.

FRANCIS HARVEY (1925 – 2014)

COWS

I watched them scratch against a lone bush,
dejected on stony hillsides in winter,
or plod in single file through summer pastures
to gape over a warped gate,
heavy-eyed at milking time, gathering.

From them I'm learning stoic simplicity:
how to gaze across a lake at dawn,
how to doze in oblivious contentment,
how to forget a calf in a week,
and, when the time comes,
how to walk proudly into a mucky trailer
and swing with dignity from a hook.

GER REIDY

SABON GIDA KANAR

The Fulani move their cattle
Onto the grassy ground
Beside the trees.

Women approach from the village
To buy milk.

The beasts settle complacently
As if this, at last, were a place
With no going onward.

PÁDRAIG J DALY

CATTLE

Up through the bowl of the evening
the cattle come in ones and twos
to where I stand at a red gate,
staring into space, not calling these cattle

who come anyway, slow and vague
at first, picking at tufts of grass,
heads and udders heavy,
coats a fresh white and black

in the half-light. Up they come
to stand in a row and stare at me,
their eyes waterbrown overlaid
with blurred and smoky blue,

their gaze modest, grave, sad.
Skin around mouths hard and moist,
grey patching a clean pink.
Odd bristles lifting, turning to light.

Black numbers stand out clearly
on yellow ear-tags. A tongue reaches
for the cold iron of the gate.
Their bodies are all touching.

Behind the row of heavy skulls,
the heavier skulls of the hills.
Fields hung like patchwork.
A thin stitching of hedge.

We stare at each other. Our breath
comes and goes, into our bodies,
back to the world, into our bodies,
back to the world, as if there were

nothing more to say, though of course
there is, always, as one cow turns
to lick a flank, one bends to eat,
slowly the rest start to wander off.

MARK ROPER

A WEATHER EYE

The afternoon a dead calf drifted to our shore
was not the first unexpected happening of the day.

The calf, bloated under vellum, her brown boots
fastened by reeds, lay with her head extended
and right eye fixed on an empty sky. Fearful.
But water is tender to the dead, and will return
what it cannot own ... eventually.

I make two calls. I tell them of the calf.
They say, *you okay?*
They say, *check its tag.*
They say, *wait.*
They say, *do nothing else 'till we're there.*

I step into the shallows, and water, sensing access,
attempts to fill my boots. As I crouch, the dead calf
lifts her head, drunkenly. She fixes on my dogs,
but they are good creatures; they sit and wait
when told. She turns her frozen gaze to mine,
tilts her head that I may see the pink serrated
edge of bone, where ear and tag
are severed. She senses the buzzards
I know are watching from their loop of sky.

Some days, exhausted by the sights daylight
thrusts upon us, we collapse early into the
bony hours of dark. The afternoon a dead
calf came to our shore was one such day,
with nothing to be done by us 'till sunrise,
and at sunrise she was gone. Wind had
changed, so water took her elsewhere.

ELEANOR HOOKER

PECK

After six years of living as a pair
one hen sickened, hunched up, as if
trying to climb back inside herself.
The other bird stood over her, on guard,
fussing, attentive, concerned, it seemed.
Close-up I could see she was pecking,
pulling out feathers around the neck
of the sick bird, baring flesh to eat.

I shouldn't have been surprised.
Everything lives off something else.
Flesh, bones, rocks, soil, selves, days,
what can they be made of but lives?
What's the great sun in all its glory
but a lustrous hen, pecking us, itself, away?

MARK ROPER

ON ENCOUNTERING A COCKROACH IN CYPRUS

My pride at getting on with spiders,
meeting mice without a bleat
comes to this fall. You
toddle towards me,
feelers waving,
my scalp ripples,
my flesh becomes a choppy sea.

Years of reading what the Buddha said,
how the Tao goes, have left their mark;

I cannot kill you
so I corral you
in the dank bathroom,
laying a towel under the door,
a blue towel but this is our green line.

All night a sinister
pottering on the other side.
Are you plotting to cross?
Mobilising more of your kind?
Obscene laughter at four o'clock
cracks the thin glaze of my sleep

and a flittered fact revisits me:
in the event of apocalypse
it's you who'll inherit the earth.

I observe the green line meticulously,
resort to the kitchen sink when I need to pee,
crossing only when the sun shows up.
There you are, small and skulking,
the colour of a blanched raisin,
paler than the richly evil shade I'd pictured.

When I look again you're gone.
I check my shoes,
rifle through my suitcase,
scuttle down the narrow stairs.

My taxi for the airport waits.
I step into silky, early air
trying to shake from my skin
prophecy's skittery patter.

KATHERINE DUFFY

'ALL ALONE AT LAST'

All alone at last –
the crab in the pool beside
the pool full of crabs.

PAT BORAN

CATCH OF THE DAY

At nightfall in the calm city the crab fishers bring
their catch, solemnly bedded on ice, to the restaurants
where starred cooks with fast practiced hands
wreathe plates with dill and bay leaves as if for a
funeral or a poetry prize. I am told that
if you sit by the water in the old harbour
with the seafarers and exiles from Genoa, Venice,
Phoenicia, a sea otter might pay you a visit,
sleek robber, native of distant kelp forests,
slowly padding up the stone steps out of the estuary's
black stinking sludge, his inquisitive
demi-god's face turning to peer in puzzlement
at the alien upper world, where all is air
and movements have little weight, looking as if
he had stepped out of some aquatic fairy tale,
the water rolling off his grey pelt
in silvered drops, his whiskers abristle in the moonlight.
If the moon nets him out at sea in its trembling mesh
of beams it will release him with the other
species of misfits, those dreamers who drift in the water
with their hands folded and their eyes on the stars.

He will send them back into the dark depths.
He will move on to find other fish to snare.

EVA BOURKE

CRICKET REVISITED

1
Cricket, hidden in a crack
of the park gate's brick wall,
all summer passing on my bike
I heard you call:
crrrk crrrk crrrk,
a creaking door, a prayer wheel.

Now all is still,
no oracular voice, no wisecrack.
The air suddenly feels cool.

Time soon
for the October moon,
fat and round as a melon
to launder gold on
the roof tiles of the town.

2
Cricket, did you know
how silent we were—how
the dog-soiled park, the sick
lindens, the dusty trick-
le in the fountain

and I on my way home
from a music-filled hall
listened to your tale
of green leaves and clear
water? How
thirsty we were?
No three-tiered choir,
no orchestra, drum, or oboe
could rival your untiring fervour.

Praise crickets and their solitary music.
Praise crevices in the brick
of park gates. Praise
dry sounds raised in intervals
of night on crumbling stone, praise
stone and night and persistent calls.

Praise the ardour of musical wings.
Praise frayed acoustic wings.
After the turmoil, the happenings,
the summer night spun on its hinge.
I heard the cricket at the gate and stood.
Praise the single note of love affirmed

in the summer night. Praise rough voices raised
to sing. Unfaltering song be praised.

EVA BOURKE

CROW CONVERSATIONS

The grey-skinned quartzite cone of the Sugar Loaf,
crows flying over, lifting towards us, flapping
in their twos and threes at first, thickening then to scores,
multitudes deepening the darkness that brings
them about. There's money in rookeries, an old voice
offers, money and luck. I grew within earshot
of crow-haunts, my dawn and my dusk crow-capped.
I saw the starveling despatched by its parents,
and a parliament convened around the diseased, to kill it.
No use in nature for weak or withered
unless to feed off, stubby maggots making the carcass
move. Still we fall over and over in love
with 'mother' nature, the 'good' earth, 'innocence'
of birds and beasts, wax lyrical in spite of all we know
of the ravening behind everything – it preys on us, too,
it scavenges – but now again the flight of crows
over the Sugar Loaf to take their rest recalls
for me far rookeries girded up out of great horse chestnut
and beech trees that stand for home, first home,
crow conversations become the earth speaking in riddles
that stay unfathomed no matter how intently I listen.

PATRICK DEELEY

CONTESTING CUCKOOS

Sumer is icumen in and I feel as if I've been living here
forever, the landscape wild as when the old
song cheering on the cuckoo was first written down,

or as if I've slipped into the sandals of that cantor
of the 13th century, his Wessex dialect – or he into mine.
Lhude sing, *cuccu;* let me accompany you.

Groweth sed and bloweth med – is that how the words go? –
and springth the wode nu. Hearty countryman,
I hear you. *Sing, cuccu!* – a few miles away to the west.

No dither or doubt, *Bulluc sterteth, Bucke
uerteth,* play it out. *Ne swic thu naver nu.* The more so
as, eager to outdo you now, a rival starts up

through the moonlit mist. The battle rolls to and fro, neck
of the wood to neck of the wood, then a lull,
a spellbound interlude; and still the living multitudes

gather and grow, the huge and heedless compulsion
of nature towards its accomplishment holds true.
Sing, cuccu, nu; sing, cuccu; Sing, cuccu; sing, cuccu, nu!

PATRICK DEELEY

ESTUARY

'Soon there will be no birds left at all,'
says the elderly man on the bench
overlooking the estuary where a dozen curlews
bend to stitch the frayed edge of blue silk.
It has been so calm, so still all day.
Maybe he is my myth visitor,
come to impart some unwanted darker news.

I sit beside him. Whatever he has read
is already haunting him, the ink
on his fingertips. We talk for hours,
until, silver-grey, the evening tide slips in
around our feet. Tonight I dream
of the last curlew flying across the estuary,
of ink stains unfolding slowly through the water.
I wake to inspect the landscape of my hands,
seeing them, as might a seabird or a drone,
so powerless, so small, so far away.

PAT BORAN

DEER

A deer met me on a lane
I didn't know –
so far ahead at the blur of ditches
and the forest slopes
that I thought at first it was a tall man
his antler height like thin arms
stretched overhead waving,
or an elegant figure suddenly stepping out,
making itself real
from an oil painting.

Both of us turned away,
afraid to stir the other's quiet.
There was only a mud way, its middle
heaped with stones between us,
only a bird more intent

on its own life warblings
half listening to our moves,
only the dull buzz of a fly agitating our silence –
and yet we felt the whole world
had stopped to watch us.

We turned away, then back again,
each fascinated by either being there,
flanked by the towering humility of trees –
the wind speeding like cars
through the highway of branches,
your ribs and mine heaving a place
in the rustling copper and silver month
we had found ourselves in.
And I understood you knew ways
I had not yet found –
envied your cool turning
into the mass of dark greens
tangling upwards to the sky,
each soft step of yours such a gentle tremor
that leaves fell in quiet reassurance,
guiding your uphill path.
If I followed, your eyes would be a light for me,
your body a blanket in the thicket of fear.
If I followed, I knew there would be
no reason to ever go back.

ENDA WYLEY

THE WILD HUNT *for Alison*

A driving holiday to the Scottish Highlands,
and on the way to Skye the road narrows and turns
serpentine, rattling the car as it coils around
the side of a fierce mountain rising from patchwork

earth like a jagged blade. The day is still and strange.
Magic light spills across the sweep of heather, gorse,
thistle and rock, blessing savage terrain with wind
bristling with rain as we ascend towards Heaven.

For a moment we are lightheaded – the laughing
gas of clouds, the bubblegum popping of warm ears –
and then we are lowered down, as if through a hole
in the burnt clay roof of the sky, where a forest,

thick as teal velvet curtains, draws back to reveal –
I hammer the brakes. A majestic stag, chewing
nonchalantly on wads of grass, stands galvanised,
antlers winking like the crown of a golden king,

flank shimmering, blocking our path to the alien
landscape beyond. He trains us with his ancient eye
for a breathless age then stands aside to allow
passage over the threshold between the two worlds.

Sometimes, as I fall asleep, I catch a fleeting
glimpse of that same eye, wet and filmy as rock pools:
the moon's oculus breaking the gap in the blinds,
permitting me entry into my borrowed dreams.

ROSS THOMPSON

RED DEER SKULL

Though it suggests the long face of a saint in a medieval
    painting,
it's still made to appear small, even incongruous,
by the many-tined antlers it bears. Antlers more rigid
    than alder,
yet full of the idea of spar and tangle as they refuse
any easy accommodation with my hands. And the red
    deer himself,
a king burdened by his crowning glory – there's that, at least,
to say to the boy who brought for classroom display
this weather-bleached specimen from where he found it,
    in a wood
near Muckross. There's the path evolution took,
turning tusks into branchy racks that – clothed with
    velvety skin –
grow in spring, and from *venari*, 'to hunt', there's venison.
But now I stand at the exit, my own semblance of solid or set
a front for all that flows. And these schoolchildren whose
    departure
I'm overseeing linger still to wrestle the skull's
primordial head-rig, to pull faces aping the empty eye sockets,
the thin 'handles' of the jawbones. Or simply to lean in
    listening
as though they can hear a last exhalation of breath,
a faint echo of the rutting season's roar. Fellow-feeling for
    a dead thing –
even a dead thing once considered a king – is not
a wonder to dwell on, but soon the houses in their pastel
    colours
materialise again, the afternoon traffic ratchets up a gear,

and somewhere in my care I rejoice at how lessons are unlearned
or broken, at how the noise and nurture run together
and sunshine in its deepening seems to promise life
    will go on forever.

PATRICK DEELEY

FETCH

Again and again she comes back to me
to place it by my feet, today's
old piece of flotsam or bonfire debris
dug out from the heap and blessed
with a kind of magic.

Dog-given, the least of things
can be treasure for a day.

And how she spends these days,
this love-struck mutt,
stretched out along a neighbour's wall,
comically shadowing the postman,
or, despite the wind and ice-flecked rain
that keeps every other dog indoors,
bounding across this desolate park
as if it were a summer's meadow, alive
to the possibility of play.

Hours, I imagine, she has spent already
running like this between her home
and mine, her world and ours,

to bring me a stick,
to chase that stick, to seize that stick
and then come back with that stick so tight
between her jaws it sometimes seems
she will never release it, that she has changed
the rules and very purpose of the game,

and had I the strength
I might lift her clear
or she might lift me clear
of this rain-locked planet.

PAT BORAN

WHO'D BE A DOG?

Who'd be a dog, who'd be a poet's dog?
When we could be up the beach digging holes,
sniffing holes, cooling the paws in the sea,

she's stuck to her iBook, worrying a line
'stars so clear have been dead for years …
stars so dead have been clear for years …'
She thinks she's it with her buttons, her plug.

It's bye-bye puppy, hello Microsoft Word;
it's laptop now where once it was lapdog.

We look so cosy, me curled at her toes,
the two of us here in the house on our own.
If she dropped down dead this instant who'd know?
Who's a good doggy then, eh? Who's the best girl?
Give or take a day or two, it'd be a week max,
before, craven with hunger, I'd start in to eat:

top o' the foodchain to you, my last mistress!
as I lick at her bare, her coolèd feet.

PAULA MEEHAN

FALSE START

I and Pangur Bán my dog.

TOM MATHEWS

TRACKS

Now my dog is dead,
paw prints in the concrete path
follow me instead.

PAT BORAN

DOLPHINS

They slip through the surface below the cliff,
two adults and a child,
rolling and folding their longed-for lengths.

We watch with two minds
this vision of fin
framed in all we now think of as loss.

Already they seem belated, shadows
of former selves,
apparitions rising from ruin.

Foam flares from their breaking backs
like words erased
as soon as they're uttered.

They rise and fall, as if trying
to mend the water.
The sea, in their wake, appears to heal.

MARK ROPER

YOUNG MAN WITH DOVES

The young man with doves
Posing for a photo
In Plaça de Catalunya

Flashes a smile
That makes him young
Until he becomes a boy again.

Joy about the birds
Perched all over him
Makes him go back

To the blind source of all delight.

PATRICK KEHOE

FLOATING

Two dragonflies, each floating
On a surf board willow leaf,

Nose to nose, those lovers
On inflated vinyl rafts,

Duellists at dawn, husband
And wife reunited at dusk.

Both can fly but don't.
This is the deepest part

Of the pond, the furthest point
From land. I'd best return.

PEGGY O'BRIEN

SHOOTING DUCKS IN SOUTH LOUISIANA

for David Tillinghast and in memory of R.C. Tillinghast

The cold moon led us coldly –
   three men in a motorboat–
down foggy canals before dawn
past cut sugarcane in December.

Mud banks came alive by flashlight.
Black cottonmouth moccasins
   –the length of a man in the bayou–
slid into black water, head high,
   cocky as you might feel stepping out on Canal Street
going for coffee at 4 a.m.
at the Café du Monde.

An Indian trapper called to us
   from his motorised pirogue,
Cajun French on his radio–
taking muskrat, swamp rat, weasel,
"anything with fur".

Marsh life waking in the dark:
gurgling, sneaking, murdering, whooping–
   a muskrat breast-stroking through weeds toward food,
his sleek coat parted smooth by black satin water–
frogs bellowing, bulbous water lilies adrift

cypresses digging their roots into water-borne ooze
dark juices collapsing cell-walls,
   oil rigs flaring thinly at daybreak.

Light dawned in our hunting-nerves.
We called to the ducks in their language.
They circled, set wing, glided into range.
Our eyes saw keener.
Our blood leaped. We stood up and fired—
and we didn't miss many that day,
piling the boat between us with mallards.

The whole town of Cutoff ate ducks that Sunday.
I sat in the boat,
bloody swamp-juice sloshing my boots,
ears dulled by the sound of my gun,—
and looked at a drake I had killed:
sleek neck hanging limp,
green head bloodied,
raucous energy stopped.
I plucked a purple feather from his dead wing,
and wore the life of that bird in my hat.

RICHARD TILLINGHAST

DUNLIN

Into the chill sea,
flock of dunlin wading out:
… *deep deep deep, deep deep* …

PAT BORAN

EEL

Eel, its serpentine
sculpture of water,
jellied steel of its back
rupturing the meniscus,
a black silk ribbon reeled
by a rhythmic gymnast,
gorgeous scoliosis in motion,
leaving the sequels
to its swim written
in ripples that keel
to each other, double
helix carved in water
darker than oil.

Boat's creel. Sargasso snakes
writhing, a greasy weave
coming to life, then the knife,
and skin peeled away slowly
with the reluctant give
of a satin elbow-length
glove, grown to love
the feel of an arm.

MARY O'DONOGHUE

ELEPHANT SKULL

Here is a strange grail indeed!
A Cyclopean vessel with teeth,
a ponderous mass
bereft of flesh and ivory.

What monstrous apparition
imbibed from this gargantuan mug
to leave it so parched

with a thirst
that all the world's tears –
past, present and to come –
will never slake?

AIDAN MURPHY

IRISH ELK

Giant antlers shine at night, diamond, sapphire, branch
in a neighbour's garden, light up the moonless dark
for children going to bed, as if the Great Irish Elk,
extinct seven thousand years, turned in his grave
beneath the lake at Lough Gur, and bellowing rose
from the bog, trailing peat from his hinds, to roam
the hills and woods of Ireland, at this time of snow
falling all across the land, on our road, ghost at
large, and twice as tall as Man come back to haunt us.

CATHERINE PHIL MacCARTHY

'FALCONS ...'

Falcons – I watch them stoop, shoot upward, thwarted.
Again and again. Hover, survey, then strike.
Down in the undergrowth small things twist and run –
mostly they escape.

Such terror in small hearts, such desperate swerve
and turn, panic, white light and breath near undone –
I feel myself project, lock, hold and retreat,
strain in every nerve,

fetching this new understanding back to thought.
Always before I had seen myself as hawk –
circling, then plunging down from the high serene
to pluck out the note

from among the roots and add it to my string.
Now everything's upside down and inside out,
I see it is not the sweeping hand that plays
but the notes that sing.

THEO DORGAN

THE FOX *for Françoise Connolly*

The fox came back, the bowl of scraps we'd left
as darkness fell licked clean
and on its side, the only sign she'd been
and gone while our small party slept

just feet away. In our pop-up dome –
by day a credible playhouse,
with dusk a thing of string and hope
shadow-insects struck like a slack drum –

we'd drifted off. Or some of us had.
For I lay awake listening for hours
in that moon-milk light – fox-time

as I think of it now – peace in the land,
my two cub scouts breathing in unison,
our makeshift den warmed by their small flames.

PAT BORAN

VIXEN

i.
Christmas night you conjured her –
turkey leavings left in a bowl by the door.

Then mornings of bones strewn like the *I Ching*.
Whatever you left was taken.

Out of winter's blue-black ink she came.
Always at night. Withheld.

It was weeks before we saw her,
a sleekness hugging shadow,

wildness, taken on form, to step into our yard.

ii.
She became our shy presence.
We'd drive home to startle her in headlights.

We raided the fridge for her, invented scraps,
only for her to retreat

and return. She brought us
the part of our selves that wasn't fully human.
Sometimes, beyond reach of the yard lamp,
she curled by the gate, waiting.

And I longed to go with her.

iii.
Spring screams set our nights on fire,
we woke to yearning tearing our paper walls,

siren cries, something like torture;
night glutted with her sounds,

we hugged each other for comfort,
awed by howl and answer –

by whatever it is that longing does
when it meets itself in the woods.

Islanded on the territory of her rut,
we were solidities her cries resounded off –

she took us into her mating,
included us, as surely other nights

we had included her.

iv.
Then silence. You abroad, so I was alone
when out from her dark gestation, she came.

She spurned me: a mistrustful slink,
back and forth over the field.

Only following her tracks, I saw them.
One after another, a litter of cubs.

v.
The young grew bold; age or curiosity
getting the better of them,

and they followed her – little ink-tipped marvels –
out of meadow grass, onto our lawn.

I tried to keep quiet, to protect them,
but there was nothing secret about their circus;

they drew the crowd, friends flocked
eager for the pleasure and wonder.

Our summer commune. Columbine, then roses,
and foxes like a blessing. We were rich with them

until the unmarked day, when the wild caught up with us –
and without warning, they disappeared.

GRACE WELLS

THE FLY

The roomful of eyes, having nowhere to look now
but into more eyes, follows the flight of a fly
in erratic orbit around the light bulb.
A chorus of neighbourhood crones stage-whispers
its comments as each new arrival crosses the floor
and an old island man with rheum in his eyes
creaks over loose boards into a chair.
The hair of the daughter who married too late
is white at the roots and Cathal from Glen
is saying how much someone I never saw
in my life before and no one else here
has ever seen darken their doors looks like himself.
178Looks like himself? That man there
who can't even raise a hand to brush off
the fly that's now settled on one white lidded eye
like the first sign of flesh reverting to clay?
The only way he'd ever look like himself
would be if he took a breath of fresh air.

FRANCIS HARVEY (1925 – 2014)

THREE LINES FOR LELAND

A housefly settles
on the still end of my pen:
haiku counterweight.

PAT BORAN

FROG SPOTTING

for Meg, Hannah, and Grace Murphy

As a ghost appears to stir the air,
The atmosphere made rarer, they appear,

Mud creatures bubbling in the muck,
A tannic stew of dead and quick.

Hard enough with cave-dwelling eyes
To spot the first star at twilight,

Let alone a troll under the bridge.
But it's sunny now and I am with

My granddaughters by the beaver pond.
Education, fun, the pedagogue's compunction

To teach the young for as long as one can
The things one thinks they ought to learn.

Like how to spot a frog. Eyes roll
As I dive into the day's lesson, not at all

Hidden: camouflage and its corollary,
The need for the eye to be predatory.

"Shhhh," I caution as my raucous gaggle
In vivid, slapping flip-flops waddles

Near the sedgy edge, so close
The goo almost oozes between their toes,

A good thing too. You have to slip through
A vestigial gill slit, plop into

A foreign element, for it to leap
Out at you, a dead thing breathing.

So, my dears, swim in the obscure,
Eyeball to eyeball decide whether

Those bulging orbs mean sight or duckweed
Froth. Alight on every lily pad.

Let it happen. Spawn vision. Verdigris
Weathered copper secreted in green

Grass, a dun fuselage in sludge,
Periscope eyes, panoramic knowledge.

Above all remember it saw you
Before you saw it. So, before we have to

Part, for my sake please, try to see
Something where nothing appears to be.

PEGGY O'BRIEN

'THE GANNETS ...'

The gannets fester with Grecian elegance
on their crude patio. Their buff of nape
and crown glows like a halo against white.
Above a broadsword of bill, eyes are glaucous,
rheumy, the eyes of old men, goggled like First War
pilots. Long shoulders, deep elbows, slope
to black tips crossed over the pointed tail.
Those standing show huge paddles of feet,
burgundy-black webs with rubber-clean
silver-blue piping that runs from the shin
over each toe. Their concerted voices
have the rhythm of corncrakes on speed.
Oh, they are active, they are social, they are
amassed. They pulverise, gather up, sweep
you with them so you bank in and down,
a parent returning to the nest with beakful
of grass or cropful of fish, gliding on albatross
wings, head tilted as your bill points your place,
feet lowered as you hang, flapping, now you're
down, the neighbours are uproarious, but your mate,
your image, is fervent with greeting. You mirror
with preening, bill-clashing, both re-staking
this rough nest, rock slab, partnership, for this
purpose: your frousled young, a caribou-grey
sack of fluff with a swarthy mask and spikish snout.
Once it was trussed in sleep; or, if awake, muzzy
with heat, gargling a pelican throat in the sun.
Now it is frantic, climbing for attention. You turn
to vomit in its maw, then back to your mate
to stroke, to nibble, to fence; to open your wings
as banners, shields, while you squawk and threaten

the neighbours who dare to hunch, to shift,
to be there. But, slowly, calm ripples back
to the eye of the storm; you may even doze,
breast and belly shading your child, your neck
swivelled, slack, so your chin rests on your mantle
and your bill, as it tracks the spine, is scabbarded
by folded wings. And now your mate rises,
swings out to where shoals river the surface,
where the purpose of the body is to circle,
focus, flatten shoulders, close like scissors,
become a spear that plunges, vanishes.

MARY MONTAGUE

GANNET

Marauder. One of a raiding party
from The Stags or Ailsa Craig maybe.
Mission today the soft target of Donegal Bay.
A painted aboriginal face
or something missing from the natural history
museum's collection of tribal masks.
El Greco at work in stained glass.
The bow that is its own arrow.
Whiter than the white the sea bleeds where he
furls himself in the water like an umbrella
pretending it's not raining in wet weather.

FRANCIS HARVEY (1925 – 2014)

FROM **GOAT**

I
Acrobats of the mountainside
high-stepping over the top
at dawn
horns wound with streamers of light.

II
No one knows like a goat
the rock's most secret chemistry
its veins of frozen salt.

III
The goat's favourite foods:
young leaves of the silver ash
the oak, birch and plantain
all types of ivy, sage, oregano
wild thyme and henbane
and every 30 days or so
it devours the whole of the moon

IV
A body of lancets and angles,
knobs, protrusions and points
and tapered joints,
ribs, pelvis and spine
arranged into one strong sweep of the neck
and gathered together in the skull's
austere Gothic design.

V

Prometheus chose the goat
as friend and helpmate.
Its eyes stare proudly
from their background of glazed gold:
stolen fire set them alight;
they have seen gods defied.

VI

What tossing of beards and locking of horns
when two rivals contend –
belligerent old men
in a parliament.

VII

The goat is horny.
The goat stinks.
The goat is capricious.
The goat is greedy.
The goat is sinful.
The goat has sex with his daughters.
it's all the goat's fault.
Let's sacrifice him to Apollo
to Priapus
to Venus
to Jehova.
Let's banish him into the desert.
Let's send him down to hell.

VIII

If two helices appear over a stonewall,
there's no need to be frightened
unless it's a midday in high summer
and they're accompanied by the sound of a reed pipe.

IX
When Böcklin painted Pan
lurking between sedge and rush
he used a few tied-together bristles
from Pan's tail as a brush.

X
He who drinks the wind.
He who breathes through his ears.
He who dreams like a human.
He who begets male offspring when the wind is southerly,
female when it comes from the North.

XI
When two goats meet on a narrow bridge
over deep water
one of them will kneel down
to allow the other
stride over it and across.

XII
Goat's meat, if sautéd, then baked in honey
spiced with bayleaves
and served in a vinegar sauce
is a powerful medicine
against epilepsy.
Ashes of a goat's horns
cure sleeping sickness;
mixed with oil of myrrh
they prevent heart disease
and underarm smells.
Ashes of a goat's hooves
are used against an inflamed anus

and loss of hair.
The blood is potent in a variety of ways:
pulverize it, mix it with the powder
of dried octopus,
pepper, thyme and wine
and it heals
all conceivable ills.

XIII
A goat was wetnurse and mother to Zeus.
Now a cluster of stars
perched on the brink of the skies
she looks down nightly
with glittering eyes.

XIV
Look at him in the bars
all girls and silken cigars
and girls and tequila
girls and guitars
gold rings and fast cars –
macho cabrillo.

XV
A kid will be a certain winner
as present for your host
at dinner,

it is also a popular first prize
in poetry or singing competitions
otherwise

you might give one to your spouse
as token of gratitude and love,
very cheap at only half an Obolus

when it takes one to pay the ferryman
to take you across the river Styx;
greedy coal-eyed Charon …

XVII
When the dead finally rise
take off their goat skins
masks and horns
wipe the blood from their faces
and go to their homes
you'll know that for the time being at least
the tragedy has ended.

EVA BOURKE

GOLDCREST

Fair enough its thin pheet-pheet in a conifer;
fair enough a glimpse of yellow crest.
But this one flew straight into this glass door
and dropped on this metal balcony at my feet,
and though I could tell it was still breathing
it had hit the glass so hard it seemed
I would just have to sit and watch it die.
I could admire the rust and buttercup cap;
the surprisingly long feathered feet. Gusts
ruffled the mud-green coat, showing grey inside.

I kept looking away, then I'd touch it
with a pencil, just to check it was breathing.
I know how inspiration comes like a bird
but this one was real, stunned, awry
on the flaking sludge-blue paint. How did it
make that mistake, not see itself coming?
Were others watching? Was it being missed?
The more I looked, the less I knew.
I turned it around, in case it woke and flew
into the glass again. Then it flew away.
No slow coming-to. It just flew, as if
it had never stopped. Vanished. Got on
with its business. So I got on with mine.

MARK ROPER

FOR MY GOLDFISH, VALENTINE

Such enormous sadness
in such a tiny world.
And, looking down at you
in the water clouded
by your flaking scales,
I wonder if my impulse
to take you home
last Valentine's Day
(following a goldfish dream)
was not just the desire
to share my tenancy
of these dusk-facing rooms
under winter's hold.

That dream of gold.

You can imagine how it took me
back into my own smaller body
and bigger, child's imagination
when I found you too incarnate
in an earlier form.
As the lama recognises
his master in a child,
entering the pet shop
I knew you then at once –
the golden fish who swam
in the lens of my parents' house,
in the lens of my childhood,
before floating up one day
to leave that world as I
too left that world, as you
soon again must leave.

Today in the meantime
you look out at me
with the same bewildered eyes,
mouthing the same mute syllable,
the eternal Om that says
nothing changes.

Lead becomes gold and gold lead.
A child will be god when god is dead.

Soon I will recognize your replacement.

PAT BORAN

TOUCHDOWN

The Brent Geese return to Bull Island

Bay, open bay, spread out below
the cloud banks, cloud-dappled, drenched
in greens and greys, scarred
by the sudden and gradual
in equal parts, but firm;

one foot-sized expanse of it,
and another beside it shimmering,
that waits for the fall of shadow,
the relaxing of muscles, the folding
of wing and reach, the dip
and careful drift down into touch
and sodden

solidity of place – the screech
of other selves, echoing of hunger,
and the ache, that sheer
collective ache, after
so much longing, so much
of nothing else to depend on
but open air.

PAT BORAN

FLEDGLINGS

Down the South Bull Wall, black guillemots
sat in a line on flat granite flags,
seven or eight – what a sight – the way
they flipped, one after the other, into air
as if a thread were pulled when the dog
fifty yards away, stopped and stared.
First, three in the water, then all
took flight over the side into the brine.
Around the lighthouse, a crescent
of fishermen, Polish, Chinese, Brazilian,
cast off the bulwark for mackerel.
On the way back, by the Half Moon,
flocks of dunlin stood on low rocks.
Buff-feathered parents nudged them off,
white-barred wings spreading.
They landed at the shore, then flew
into the air as if one body, gliding along
a breaker, changing formation.
Now on the estuary, in the flow,
three black guillemots bobbed about,
and low, and behold, down the quay wall
leaning out of her crevice-nest,
the mother bird called to them
as they trailed the youngest
that playfully dipped its head,
dived into the deep and surfaced.
She, all the while attentive, called them
off the swift, outgoing current
that threatened to sweep them away,
urged them, and called them in, to safety.

CATHERINE PHIL MACCARTHY

GIORRIA ARTACH   *IÚL, 2003*

Id staic i logán sléibhe, do dhá chluas
Ar bior, d'fheadfá bheith san airdeall
Ar ghlam gadhar i ngleannta Uíbh Ráthaigh,
Ach go scéitheann dath aolbhán do chóta

Gur sneachta an tuaiscirt is dual agus dúchas duit.
Nó an é an bainne a ghoid an chailleach,
Á dhiúl i riocht ghiorria ó bhuaibh na gcomharsan,
A chlaochlaigh thú go gile sin na gcríoch seo?

Cuma sa tsioc. San iarghúltacht chrua seo
Leánn agus reonn rógaireacht agus leochaileacht
Tríd is tríd a chéile, beag beann ar chora
Tromchúiseacha an tsaoil. Teacht slán is cúram.

Tásc ná tuairisc níl agamsa le coicíos
Ar an saol mór ná ar chinnithe na bhfear
A labhrann le Dia is a labhrann Dia leo
Roimh scaoileadh na mbuamaí, roimh an gol san ár.

Ach ó tá an domhan mar ghiorria idir chonartaibh,
Gach aon bhall ar crith, ag éisteacht faoi sceimhle
Le séideadh adhairce na sealgairí mire
Ar shliabh is ar mhachaire is ar fhásach,

Seo mo ghuí do ghiorria i logán sléibhe sa Ghraonlainn:
Fiolar, faolchú ná ulcabhán nár thaga ort,
Crobh, gob ná fiacal nár ruga riamh ort,
Is ná raibh do chlúmh bán choíche breac led fhuil.

PADDY BUSHE

ARCTIC HARE *JULY, 2003*

Transfixed in a mountain hollow, your ears
All attention, you could be listening out
For baying beagles in Uíbh Ráthach valleys,
Only your lime-white coat cannot conceal

That northern snow is in your blood and breeding.
Or is it the milk that the old witch, taking
The shape of a hare, stole from the neighbours' cows,
Has you morphed into this indigenous brightness?

No matter. In this unyielding remoteness,
Villainy and vulnerability meld one
Into the other, undisturbed by the weighty
Ways of the world. Survival's the thing.

For two weeks now, I've had neither sight nor sound
Of the big world, nor of the decrees of men
Who speak to God and to whom God speaks
Before the bombs' release, the weeping in the slaughter.

But since the world is now a hare between packs,
Trembling in every part, listening in terror
To the bugling of the crazed hunters
Among mountains and plains and deserts,

Here is my wish for this hare in a Greenland hollow:
May no wolf nor owl nor eagle come upon you,
May no tooth nor beak nor talon tear you,
And may your white fur never be dappled with blood.

PADDY BUSHE

THE HARE

Somewhere between
Drogheda and Dunleer
I saw a leggy hare
crossing an open field;
the train seemed slowed
to the animal's lope,
his ancient shape-
shifting, unrequited traipse
to the cover of trees.

But in the time it takes
a gaze to angle,
steady, aim,
the hare and I weren't there –
his life, my life, lost
in the lick of wheels
on track, that instant
velocity of always
elsewhere.

ENDA COYLE-GREENE

HUNTING DOGS, HARES AND FROGS

Late September
and I'd left my desk
to stroll by the lake,
the orange path
crunching underfoot,
the air grown clear
from a risen mist.

Then the hoarse alarm
of a jackdaw's *kaaaarr,*
and I heard them howl,
those hunting dogs come
after work, chasing
the hares through
the forest dark.

Out onto the rolling green
the petrified hares came
preparing to drown
themselves in fear.
But the frogs, afraid
of them, leapt into
the dense lake first.

And I remembered
the fable –
*By the water's edge
the wise hare knows
there's always
someone*
worse off than him

ENDA WYLEY

HEDGEHOG

On those nights,
not lit by any moon
through Malahide
along the coast,
past Howth,
the city stood
against the dark –
so many strands
strung with diamonds
resting on a plain
black dress.

Our house lights
shaped an up-turned boat
out of two Nissen huts
welded together,
it seemed to float
over marram
and scutch;
beyond the fence
the real sea touched
and kept touching
sand.

Wrapped in each other
and in our walk,
we were back
in the garden
when I noticed driftwood
you almost kicked –
but it glittered,

had eyes set into
a coat of spines, a body
we would nourish
with bread, milk, time.

ENDA COYLE-GREENE

THE KILL

The tai chi of the heron,
As she ballet trawls
Crepuscular for supper.

The soundless breeze of lifting
One, Angle-poise, lead
Leg after another.

Knife insertion, blade clean
Strokes, slow motion rowing
Over a pond of patience.

Everything is preparation,
Learning to endure
The atmosphere of living

Underwater. Feather
Breaths that stick like rocks
In a constricted throat,

Interminable neck,
The length of time despair
Can take before it fish flashes

Look, here, hunger,
Something smaller but better
Than wishing you were dead.

PEGGY O'BRIEN

EGRETS IN THE TOLKA

Today one takes flight
from the shingle spit
beneath the Luke Kelly Bridge,

sweeps its blizzard wings
around the Esso station,
over the Jewish cemetery,

to the back of the Poplar Row flats –
swingsets empty
on a Sunday morning –

above me, the happenstance
of hollow bone, dusty thermal,
becomes an aerial show

by a bird that looks through me,
seeking only the shadows
of slow-moving fish.

JESSICA TRAYNOR

HERON

in memory of Beatrice Behan

was assembled out of bits and scraps, not made.
Like one of those early flying machines held together
    with glue and twine.
His undercarriage is an afterthought sticking out behind.
He is all wings and no fuselage and probably hollow inside.
Finn could have blown him off the palm of his hand.

He creaks into flight. The wind buffets him, gives him
a bumpy ride: it seems he must somehow end up
in a twisted heap of canvas and struts on the mountainside.
But no: he tacks into weathers with a prow that rises
    and falls in the swell.
The ghost of the pterodactyl haunts him in every cell.
He alights: furls his wings like a wet umbrella, settles,
    rapt and murderous,
drying out in the wind and sun on the edge of a tarn
or hunched over a pool in the burn pretending he's
a blind one-legged beggarman or a mystic
    communing with God.
Too late, too late for the fish or frog when it realises
    he's not an old cod.

Heron invented slow motion long before the movies came but
allows himself the lightning of his pickaxe for the killing game.
Heron's the icon of the silences beyond the last tongues
of land where the islands float and quiver like mirages in
    the light,
he's the hermit who daily petrifies himself in the reeds
    of the penitential lake,
the logo of the lonely places past the last sheep and

the last house,
the El Greco or Modigliani doodle in a remote corner
     of the evening sky where
the newsprint of distant waders swims before the eye,
heron's that sudden outlandish screech you hear at midnight
in the water meadows as he changes into the wrong gear.

FRANCIS HARVEY (1925 – 2014)

HERON

Every now and then, often at dusk,
as if to darken the darkness of dark,

over the house a heron wrings out
its terrible cry: a note, long pondered,

exactly the same as all preceding, all
to come, to add to that lifelong solo

whose scale, slowness, lack of closure,
whose unchanging survey and sum of sorrow

and sadness and sadness and sorrow,
whose utter lack of meaning and hope

make even the most heart-rending lament
seem child's play, merest self-pity.

MARK ROPER

COMMON HERON *for Mark Roper*

Natural History Museum, Dublin

Ruffled, dishevelled,
all claws and stilts,
a somewhat bewildered stare,
I'm grey-downed and -feathered,
a creature stepped out of a fog
wrapped in a cape;
entranced, intent,
reading the curving lines
in the wood of my case
like tracks in the sand,
rivulets caressing, inscribing
the estuary grains;
and darkness arriving
any time now, so they say,
but my bill's steely tip
is still steady,
still poised at the ink-well of night,
still ready to dip.

PAT BORAN

HERRING GULLS

The herring gulls distract. They stand like courtiers
primed to your movements: jealous; opportunist.
Their stare whets the sound rolling over the headland,
urging you rise and track that harsh babble, which grows

as you climb and follow across rough sheep-cropped
herbage that edges the tundral Barrens. From the air
some gulls keep with you, but now, as you near
the top, they yield to gannets, a grander escort
with their black isosceles of wingtip,
their symmetry of heron-bill, hypodermic tail.
An acid tang of guano scours your pharynx,
flavours the gathering noise, which like the roar
of the crowd at the crucial moment, breaks
as you crest the rise. Land slips away, an open palm;
and there between thick splayed digits, the stack
of Bird Rock. Jostling gannets make a ragged
icefloe on top. The flanking cliffs are spattered
with terraced thousands. Overhead, white
purity of seabird is like a call to clean living, to pare
to essentials, the streamline of *eat; reproduce*.
Here, where land gives out is a tenemented
township of believers: gulls, gannets, kittiwakes;
murres, guillemots, razorbills. A steaming metropolis.
The air holds a chaos of traffic, wheeling, milling,
to confuse all sight. The cacophony routs all thought.
You go to the edge. Bird Rock is just a leap away.

MARY MONTAGUE

HORNETS' NEST

A paper lampshade, but many times layered, at the tip
of whose warm, plump cone no bulb peeps,
only a small black aperture designed for entry and exit.
The flat base is glued, not hung, above our heads,

in the boilerhouse. Summer gave us no reason
to potter here. Now we're too late to see the hornets.
But taking heart from wonders which the world,
if it ever stops to think about them at all, might call
insignificant – earthworms gowned in a froth
of mating, earwigs hatching and nestling their young,
or those grasshoppers we met in a Wicklow glen,
hosts unwary enough to let us touch off them – we cherish
the elaborate, empty nest, the notion of a lampshade
wrought from regurgitated bark, flowers, sap;
we envision nature as living lights that range forever out.

PATRICK DEELEY

ANATOMY OF THE HORSE

What made George Stubbs decide to make
the horse his subject? To choose a creature
of utility and show it worthy of the same
respect as any classical god or ideal form?
A focus on horseflesh so consummate, paint
so animate, the story goes that Whistlejacket himself
reared up at his own image. After years
as a jobbing portraitist, when he came to his modest
inheritance, the man left wife, children, his familiar
trade, for this madness: to hole up in a Lincolnshire
barn with carcases now dignified as 'horse cadavers';
to slowly strip layers of flesh to its bone. Months
on each corpse. Years in total. A decade distilled
to *The Anatomy of the Horse in Eighteen Tables*
all done from Nature. It is A particular Description
of the Bones, Cartilages, Muscles, Fascias, Ligaments,

Nerves, Arteries, Veins and Glands that omits
the gore, rot, stench, flies, the risk of disease,
to yield – chalked, pencilled, inked, etched –
clean dissected glory. What does it say, this intemperate
looking, this practised *knowing* of an animal
from the marrow out? That earnest laborious
devotion to detail, worship of the gritty factual,
is love. George Stubbs loved horses;
not lightly, easily, sentimentally;
but brutally, culpably, viscerally,
unashamedly; heart, blood and sinew.
And every touch of paint betrays
the depths he would reach to,
the heights transcended.

MARY MONTAGUE

A TALE OF HORSES

Horses looming out of the mist below
And disappearing upwards again,
A steel shoe ringing here and there
On a rock, abrupt scramblings
At a stream, uneasy snorting
And we also uneasy, strained,
Awkward in our saddles, the mountain
Swaying around and below us
In the fog, then up and again up
And away back into story.
What raid is this, what Viking
Plundering of the valleys,
What bloody epic is being composed,
What Eric the Red's fame narrated,

What story, what saga,
What Arctic winter's tale is this?

All of a sudden, then, with a jerk
Of reins and hooves and minds,
We're up and out, the mist below us,
And around and around and around,
The unfiltered brilliance of the peaks
Stretching themselves icily
To the four corners of the earth,
Summit after summit supremely careless
Of us, of our hearts in our mouths,
Our mouths agape in mute wonder,
And we are stone deaf to any story
Ever recounted since time began.

PADDY BUSHE

HOUSE MARTINS

we start like rain start like rain
one or two then one and two

then everywhere for hours air
round with us with us and ours

our scrawl of smalt and stringing inks
our skift and skirr and skreel

the heat and seethe and stink of us
a bound noun all speed and wheel

MARK ROPER

HUMMINGBIRD

Not just how
it hung so still
in the quick of its wings,
all gem and temper
anchored in air;

not just the way
it moved from shelf
to shelf of air,
up down, here there,
without moving;

not just how it flicked
its tongue's thread
through each butter-yellow
foxglove flower
for its fix of sugar;

not just the vest's
electric emerald,
the scarf's scarlet,
not just the fury
of its berry-sized heart,

but also how the bird
would soon be found
in a tree nearby,
quiet as moss at the end
of a bare branch,

wings closed around
its sweetening being,

and then how light
might touch its throat
and make it glow,

as if it were the tip
of a cigarette
smouldering
on the lip of a world,
whose face,

in the lake's hush
and the stir of leaves,
might appear,
for a moment,
composed.

MARK ROPER

THE KESTREL

is quartering the hill all day with murderous intent.
There is something up there whose heart will never relent.

Look how it rides the vicious swell that rocks it in mid-air.
A fierce rapt contemplation is brooding on something
        up there.

The mouse shivers in the shadow shivering on the grass:
The only cloud in the rain-scoured sky that will never pass.

Something utterly true to itself, a stone being a stone,
Is plunging into its shadow and the mouse's flesh and bone.

Is it the inexorably professional way it is done
Earns accolades from the larks melting into the sun?

FRANK HARVEY (1925 – 2014)

'TSK, TSK, TSK, POOR YOU ...'
FROM 'OUTBACK HAIKU'

'Tsk, tsk, tsk, poor you,'
the most sincere regrets of
the bush kangaroo.

IGGY MCGOVERN

SLEEPING WITH THE KINGFISHER

Its appearance in the bed wasn't surprising.
Giraldus said a dead one kept linen fresh.

No, what surprised was the size of the thing
and the way it hugged me close to its breast.

To feel its bill run the rule down my spine.
To be enfolded in sapphire wings. Surprising.

How much more so to wake and find myself ablaze,
my heart the blue seed in a blossom of flame.

MARK ROPER

A DREAM OF LAPWINGS

All day, as we walked the island,
Lapwings cavorted in the wind, or carried
Their crested silhouettes from rock to rock,
Mewing between heather and sheep-cropped grass.

You once dreamed, you said, of a great lapwing
That with huge wingbeats and rippling plumage
Carried you high over familiar mountains
While you clung to the iridescence of its crest.

Later, as we lay drowsily
High among the cliff-top buttercups,
Lapwings in high-pitched abandon above us
Played your dream again. I could see

The hugeness of your flight above a valley,
How it brought people streaming out of doors
To marvel at the shadow, and to feel
The beneficence of those passing wings.

PADDY BUSHE

SCRIBBLE LARK

How strange these lanes and hedgerows still
appear, making me want to look
deeper into them. The spider spinning a silk
sarcophagus about a wasp, tendering it
to a potential mate. The fern drawing on mist
to bless its fertilisation. The rat's burrow,
freshly earthed – but there's a wagtail

squatting in it now, having cosied the interior
with moss, a feisty little warrior
prepared to battle for hours, using the narrow
opening to hold the returned rodent off.
Sometimes I think I'm mad, leaning
past dusk, fascinated as the runny-nosed child
who long ago started the neighbours
wondering. My world is burning down, being
blown down, withering, drowning,
but on nights of deep freeze the wrens gather
as they have always done, a ball
of them rolled into one simply to keep warm,
while in spring the long-eared owl alights
on the spruce-tree nest accumulated by crows
and outsits their furore, or in another
scenario a yellowhammer warbles to his partner
the songs learned from his father
in the idiom and accent of this place; for here
is nature, working with its own will;
and here she sits – the 'scribble lark', hatching
a clutch of scribble-marked eggs, in
the rusted exhaust of an old tractor in a sawmill.

PATRICK DEELEY

HAIKU FOR BONNIE *after Lorca*

The lizard asleep
one droplet of crocodile
on a yellow leaf.

GERRY MURPHY

LUGWORM

If I could join together these pieces
of string heaped on the beach I'd have a line
long enough to fly a kite to heaven
or plumb the ocean's deepest abysses.

FRANCIS HARVEY (1925 – 2014)

MACKEREL

line no sooner down than taut
    shadow silvering into air
desperate fruit all wriggle
    and twitch snapped off
slapped in a plastic crate
    fading to layers of leaves
knives out guts chucked
    to an instant coven of gulls
heads scarfed whole
    sea a boil of snatch and scream
fillets home in a bucket
    fried in their own oil
all night my head full
    of saltwater skin sun
flesh feather beak bone
    so little between us

MARK ROPER

MAGPIE

The day builds itself piece by piece;
the newt joins the owl, then the porcupine,
quince on its branch bends over a ruby ring,
colour seeping across the living room floor

until the jigsaw's yacht sails to its zebra end
and we go walking, your hand a small ball
in my palm poised to roll where adventure hides
in parks, wild gardens, up doorsteps, behind pots.

Your eyes, beady berries on Raymond Street's trees,
see everything – and then, just there, *muck-pie,*
muck-pie, you call to the bird that tussles
with the daffodils, that pecks for sparkling light

like diamonds through the railings. Our day
building and renewing will not stop.
Blueberries devoured, cod stew and sleep
the warm milk of waking, later the afternoon

becoming a city of wooden blocks up to the ceiling –
only the great moon in the sky and the twinkling star
will drag you in song from your industry.
Then night has you nestling close to my neck,

your lips whispering the day's things softly.
Muck-pie, muck-pie, your energy pulling
at the jade on my chain feels relentless to me –
like the jay all ready to steal and fly away.

ENDA WYLEY

MAGPIES

might have once been part of some fabulous
operetta irretrievably lost
in transit and now whirring raucously

about our dazzling sets and backdrops
like wound-up mechanical props on the loose
and about to run out of power but

there's nothing operatic about them when,
hopping mad on the road round splatters
of squashed guts and bones, they pick the tarmac

clean again or when a lone one crosses
the path of Mary Bridget on her way
to the well and stops her dead in her tracks.

FRANCIS HARVEY (1925 – 2014)

FRIDA AND THE MONKEYS

after a painting by Frida Kahlo

Frida sits on the veranda of her blue house,
eyes fixed on the giant orchid poking
from a stone jar before her. The flower
is a buttery yellow, its fleshy outer whorl
enclosing an ochre throat striped with ruby –
the mouth of a cave lined with tiger skin.
She sits, bolt upright, her broken spinal column
clamped in a steel corset that spikes her ribs.

Two favourite spider monkeys squat
on her downy forearms, their long arms
stretching round her shoulders, wizened
hands cupping the back of her neck.
Their mouths are fixed in a solemn moue,
their black eyes, like hers, stare at the plant.

Sounds of a band break over the wall.
The monkeys twitch and flick their tails
at red cactus flowers, sleeping parrots
leave the shade of the jacaranda and flap
at shuttered windows as kettle drums
and shrieking cornets lead a frayed gang
of clowns and rope-walkers into the alley-way
beyond the house. Frida cannot see them
but she knows them, knows the double-bass,
the little bassoon and the big bassoon, the oboes
and green ivory hunting-horns, the bagpipes
and fipple-flutes, knows the caterwauling,
the banging on her ear-drums, knows the dwarf
woman, her perfect woman-sized feet kicking
and stomping and jerking the band forward.
Frida closes her eyes, opens her lips
her mouth, her ruby throat. A howl
ricochets off the garden wall, scattering
monkeys in trees.

MARY NOONAN

A.M.D.G. *

This April morning, moorhen,
I'm glad to see you glide
Along the sunny grand canal
On your black backside.

Where the water willows lean
Down from the lawns
You navigate a deeper green
Among the sleepy swans,

And bring me so much happiness
The busy city's sound recedes
A moment from my consciousness
Until you vanish in the reeds.

TOM MATHEWS

JAWS

Encountering the corpse stiff in the trap,
This scrap whose mousecrap fouled my pots and pans,
I stoop to throw him out.
His bloodied snout
Sets me the question how (to coin a phrase)
My best laid plans are getting on these days.

TOM MATHEWS

* *Ad maiorem Dei gloriam* / To the greater glory of God

THE SONG THE ORIOLE SANG

As if our Dante Alighieri
in his *Purgatorio* or *Paradiso*
went on about a recipe
for puttanesca,
or recommended a Nearco wine,
why, in long lines
and many volumes, does Bai Juyi
recount for us particulars
of boiling up bamboo shoots
with rice, and how,
on waking from his nap late afternoon,
he took two cups of special tea?

He was a mandarin
who governed provinces,
was sometimes in and sometimes out,
but in the midst of this he tells us more
about the price of peonies
twelve hundred years ago
in the Imperial City,
about the song the oriole sang
as the administrator paused
from drafting papers,
than anything those papers might have said.

So I had thought,
until I saw the commentary in portraits:
self-mutilating soldiers,
the woman gleaning the grain
her family must live off,

the old farm labourer who bows his head
passing the flower-stall, to think,
"A cluster of deep-red flowers
would pay the tax of a whole family."

So now, within vicissitude,
I study with Bai Juyi
the frontier-free coherent universe
of plum-tree or cherry-branch,
would strive with him
towards temples
air-cooled by altitude
at six days' walk from the familiar river
or stop – for what
to peasant or poet pausing here
a thousand years before
the river magisterially gave.

PHILIP McDONAGH

OTTER

Some things happened that should not have,
I made mistakes and was given witness to my worst self –

I was left like something a spider leaves,
sucked of everything except despair.

We founder and must find ways to mend.
One foot in front of the other I walked the riverbank,

inland, upstream, letting water flow against my failings.
I struck a path through cow-parsley and nettle,

holding the indigo lamp of bluebells to my damage,
moving deeper toward the river's quiet country,

further into my personal ruin. Where the two
converged I slumped among the wet weeds, wanting

the river to wash right through me, to wipe me clean.
And up from the liquid surface rose an otter;

an otter plunging the water. It dived to somersault,
to divide in two and become a mated pair.

Black as eels but halo-bright they circled, swimming
me into their carnival, into a wider world –

so that I want to say, do not fear your anguish;
despair births miracles; hope is only waiting for release.

Pay attention, the signs gifted are subtle: small beads
for the necklace of faith we must thread for ourselves.

GRACE WELLS

OWL

Its soft feathers achieve a silence
That barely disturbs the dark.
Its body, in between its outspread wings,
Is a fluffy thing a child might cuddle,

Not knowing that all this quiet
Covers a heart ordained
To search for small lives in the night,
To swoop and kill.

PÁDRAIG J DALY

HALLOWEEN OWL

Before the Gaelic pitch was a Gaelic pitch,
it was a pitch-black hole full of every frog and vole
that ever plashed in moonlit pools.

I can't be sure it was an owl
but, one night, late, already scared,
I saw the false-face tilted down.

Cailleach Oíche. Hag of Night.
Gloom-bird to the poet Keats,
and tonight I saw it on my Dublin street.

It's a foolish man believes in omens,
but like a decent Roman I should have nailed it
    to the door,
a wreath to ward against the meaning of itself.

I took it for that childhood bird,
not so much for what it was
as for the utter nothingness I heard.

JOHN KELLY

ORNITHOLOGY IN DOHENY AND NESBITT'S

It was dark in the bar that night, but we were talking
about the day-lit owl that flashed through branches
overhead as I drove to the gate – not a flicker

in its reach, more of an expanse than I would have thought
possible, I said – and you agreed that neither one of us had
ever seen an owl except as drawn from life, as wooden

as the key-ring fob brought back to me from Greece, its
belly etched in red ink with my initials and my mobile
number, my personal talisman.

I couldn't understand why seeing it had made me happy,
as if the rush of beating wings had somehow owned the
power to break my heart, or make it whole,

and I told you how I'd listened to the same sound
grounded, stinging in its frantic uselessness within walls; in
the guileless air outside, another country, a blessed galaxy

it escaped to through the sudden ardent softness of an
open window. Later, as I'd waited for the light to leave
the sky – not lonely, I said, not really, just quiet –

in the space between what is safe and what might
only be described as sinister, other voices, other birds,
tricked kindness off the witch-dense, painted woods;

above the rest, the echo-stressed vocabulary of the
cuckoo calling time across a distance left me with no
sense of what its message meant, if it had one,

if it was an omen like the owl was once for Rome, or a
piseog – a malevolence swept into panicked wings that
have been trapped indoors –

you wondered too: you said you didn't know, but I kept
asking, asking, thinking of a hawk I've never spoken of,
that tested gravity on air while all below was melded

to an under-map of moss on stone, the warp and weft
of meadow grass. I watched it for what seemed to me
the longest breath I've ever held before the spell broke

open and the world became an island, its beaches
chalked outlines around a body: I'm still not certain
why it dived, or how or when it was

that I had realised its eyes – like flinting glass in
sunlight sharpened all that swift way down – could
see the shape of everything, the state of me.

ENDA COYLE-GREENE

GIANT PANDA

There was excess postage on the package
for the *Musée d'Histoire Naturelle*
Père David sent back from China
in 1896. Out of it fell

a monochrome pelt,
a skeleton and a few lines about amazing weeks
in the Himalayas, finding a raccoon-faced lumberer
in woods amid jagged peaks.

The bear with its dark spectacles in a white face,
the priest with his cassock, white collar and air of distinction,
both camouflaged in the dapple sun on snow,
all light and shadow, loners on the brink of extinction.

A carnivore turned vegetarian, barely surviving
on its own bodyweight of bamboo,
a missionary no longer converting the native gods
into something palatable. Poor you:

Stuck between opium wars and bouts over tea,
your specimens damaged by assistants who didn't care,
the music you hated, the burden of trunks and cases,
your golden monkey skins perishing in the humid air:

Before you return to Tientsin, where the Christians are dead,
ten Daughters of Charity murdered, your mission house
    blazing,
if only everything could stop at this moment that knows
nothing but the quiet eyes of a new bear, gazing.

CATHERINE ANN CULLEN

STORM PETREL *for Éibhear, in welcome*

For six months I kept *Blackbird* hidden, safe,
While worms of hope fattened. Now your newly
Over-the-moon father rightly says it needs
A sequel. But I find a blackbird too ordinary,
Too banal, however sweet, to be correlative
Enough for your tiny momentousness.
The wings that beat instead into my mind
Are those of storm petrels, nightbirds on Skellig,
Whose gurglings in walls and crevices by day
Were a warm promise, never fully realised
Until the birds whizzed past me in the dark
And torchlight guided me to where they perched,
Newly landed, impossibly frail in the face
Of all that wind and weather, bearing within
Their restless eyes and tiny quivering frames
The knowledge of the oceans, of the stars.

PADDY BUSHE *(See 'Blackbird', p. 21)*

THE PHEASANTS

They perch upon a papier-mâché rock,
eternal calm before the beater's cry,
retrievers, plus-fours, cartridge-belt and stock,
both barrels peppering the autumn sky.

The taxidermist, Williams of Dame Street,
recalls to still life feather, beak and claw
(rare bird himself where Art and Science meet,
also a celebrated concert draw.)

Observers of the Big House rise and fall,
bought for ten shillings at the closing sale,
willed on to us, as if in answered call,
and once again they take the southern trail.

The well-worn ties of time and place are loosed
as more than these two birds come home to roost.

IGGY McGOVERN

PIGEON OUTSIDE THE DEAD WOMAN'S HOUSE

Like a casual passer-by
She strolls, her shawl
Of feathers neatly pinned.

Outside Theresa's cottage
She picks at the crumbs
Of the old woman's soul.

Maybe takes it on loan.
When life peters out like that
There's no certainty

Of who is who, whether
Theresa is the pigeon
Or the pigeon is Theresa.

It is true that Theresa,
When still living,
Gazed at the island,

The island of her birth
Perhaps thinking
Were I a bird

I'd give it a peck,
A peck of a kiss,
Just there and back.

So maybe the pigeon
Is just hanging around
For instructions.

LELAND BARDWELL (1922 – 2016)

PIKE *for Pat Lunny*

Near Devenish, the boat tied sideways
to a golden screen that would cut the hand off you –
and yet was soft and featherheaded too –
I saw a scene in silhouette as unbelievable to me
as Viking ghosts or risen Christs.

A pike was plashing in the shallows –
out of its depth entirely – and a water-hen
was riding on its back, attacking fins and gills
and giving out yards in its own astonishment.
It was surely some mirage or wishful thought?

But then the trembling reeds began to part
and, just beneath the surface, the pike,
perplexed by impulse, emerged just inches from the boat
to hang there like a mottled log,
hints of wolfish gold and silver in the light.

With one hand I could have lifted it clear,
held it heavy and sky-high.
But with not a one to see it happen, I held instead
it's sinking misbelieving glare
as, slowly, I began to shimmer, rise and fly.

JOHN KELLY

RATS

There's always rats, even at beauty spots
like Sandymount Strand,
where the trouser legs of Bloom shuddered
at the sight of Gerty's upper thighs.
Those rocks are rife with rats, and labyrinthine.

And that shop window in the first Arrondissement,
in Rue des Halles where dead rats hung
all-noosed as I wandered back to the Métro.
Every night I saw them gnawing upwards into death.
To a sweaty afterlife of trouser legs and flesh.

JOHN KELLY

RAVENS

never had a good press, infesting
old lays and legends long after
they'd finished off Cuchulainn like

daylight Transylvanian bats or
transmogrified witches, two black
hags flapping heavily about the glens
day after day cracking their gallows
jokes, trailing a sick lamb or
a stricken fox, picking the eyes out
of the living and the dead. Only
last week I saw a pair shadowing
an old man out after sheep on Suhill.
Pity poor Con the undertaker
if they took a fancy to him.
Ravens are real eye-openers.

FRANCIS HARVEY (1925 – 2014)

RHINO

Commotion at the water-hole as he approaches,
a shuffling of armour scattering the dust.
Nervy gazelles skitter at the edge as
he stomps into the shallows, past

flusters of flamingos, the little tick bird
lording it on his back. A square-lipped
scowl lowered; from the still water is heard
a guzzling and a greedy gulping, lusty god

in robes of crumpled iron. Above him
parakeets jeer but keep their distance,
this muddy basin his brute kingdom
till he's sated. Bush-shadows, inference

of voices; the great head lifts and turns,
scenting the air. Once these porthole eyes
watched dinosaurs like super-tankers roam the plains.
But now he blinks, straining in the haze

to shape the blurs that stare back
from leaf-light as he sniffs once more, inhaling
the sweat-soaked shirts, the oily reek
of gunmetal. Warning screeches in the wing-

flapped air, but there's no holding him,
the terrible head-spikes angled for the charge.
Thunder underfoot, but all he hears is the blood-drum
bang in brain as he rumbles in grey rage

into the barrel-flash, smoke rising from the muzzle,
then staggers in a slow-motion capsize.
One last bewildered moan. Becomes history, huge fossil
as the men advance, wary at first, then later cries

of triumph. The dull clack of machete blade;
overhead the vultures fly a holding pattern.
On the ground the horns wait to be mounted,
each one a sad lopped-off erection.

JOHN O'DONNELL

THE ROBIN

For days it kept on tapping at the window,
a spent coal trying to regain a fire,

a little glowing boat beating against
a wall of surf, a frozen sheet of spray.

When we opened the window, in it flew.
Began, it seemed, to search, as if for what
had been there when it was out, but now
was out when it was in. Soon it was tapping

at the window again, from the inside, as if
the real thing was to cross that barrier,
as if the real world lay beyond
and it were living in a realm of shadow.

When you read it was after its reflection,
thinking it a rival, or a partner,
we saw that image growing in its head,
an ideal bird in an ideal space, we saw

the little robin storm the gates of heaven
and find itself bewildered and alone,
finding that heavens depend upon not
being entered, there being no other side.

We might have seen it homeless then, flying
back into a world suddenly strange,
provisional, a stage set to be ransacked
for hints of another, better place –

but it flew straight into its world, its home,
straight into its struggle and its song.
In the window, looking on, we saw ourselves:
in our minds that glass, that image entered.

MARK ROPER

THE ROOKS' RETURN

In cold-season dusk
they are an explosion of homecoming.
The starved arms
of the bare trees are stretched
to reach them.
The leaf litter
is spattered with their uric graffiti.

You stand there,
a small tree yourself,
as condensing twilight
flattens, blurs, the surrounding shapes
and the sky drains
to a chilled darkness-blue.

You hear, at first, a distant chuckle,
a lapping tide, that amplifies, approaches
as a rasping corvid chorus. You see them,
as you've seen them other evenings from the hill
above the woods, like a black river, like a splay
flowing inwards and downwards to converge
on this hub of the forest, the belly in which you stand.

And they come carping, having seized their day
and now full of rough talk about it. As the witching
capes of their wings pell-mell over the treetops,
they shout their arrival, their right of way
with harsh masculine laughter, and you,
caught in their boisterous commuter confusion,
surge at their streeling vortex. They drop
so the trees, tufted, become hotch-potch
candelabra. The tufts holler

to familiar strangers, jostle and squawk
to take possession of a favourite roost
and settle in for the night,
drunk on each other's presence,
raucous with tales of the day:
warmth that sustains
until dawn.

MARY MONTAGUE

RETURN OF THE SALMON

after Ted Hughes's 'Night Arrival of Sea Trout'

All night I waited.

Early mist and rowan berries scarlet
in the waking stream announced

their coming like a telegraph.
In dawn light the earth sang beneath her breath.

Hazel-nuts tumbled from her skirts
and the larks ran on ahead,

carrying her tune above the moor
and downstream

to the stubble fields and the Horned God
running, leaping with his drum.

GRACE WELLS

FROM **SCORPIONS**

I built a castello of stones and mud
and great baulks of seasoned timber
with oak doors in the walls
and then I whitewashed the walls on the inside
put a fire-back and pots in the fire-place
a new-forged crane and hooks and chain
and in preparation for the siege ahead
I laid in logs and charcoal
onions and oil and garlic
and sides of bacon hanging from the beams
and then I sat back and waited
this whole peninsula was waiting
and I was European and waiting for the Barbarians …

And in the end like dreams they came
black scorpions came down my walls to join me
finding recognition in the whites of my eyes
soot creatures from before my childhood
from that rain-streaked chimney space
black scorpions came down my white-wash walls
and I know the limits of this farm-house hearth
what people occupied this place
my grandmother's bedroom stretching away
away from the house and the hill and the furze
my dead uncles standing like frozen horses
and the beasts that stamp and knock beneath
and I am European and waiting for the Barbarians

MACDARA WOODS (1942 – 2018)

THE SEALS AT MILL BAY, RATHLIN

Dark black and brown and grey
dappled pelts soaking,
lazing and luxuriating in the sun,
still and stretching,
fatty sculptures, sea-made,
salt-nourished, below the disused
kelp store. Bladder-wrack
and long tangle drying in the sun.
A rusted anchor lodged
into the soil beside briny
black lobster pots. They lounge
and bathe and buoy themselves up
to watch, caretakers among
the throng of building.
The sun's light dispersing,
mottled on the water, shimmering
like the cobweb on the windowsill,
holding fast its thin frayed
filaments set shining below
a trinity of windmills. Barking,
majestic mythical creatures,

I imagine the lost diver among you,

his friends' false skins discarded,
slung over the harbour railings
like seals who've left their bodies
to become seducing humans.
Wet suits disembodied,
masks and breathing apparatus,
fins and snorkels laid out.

The wreck he dived into empty,
the oxygen canisters empty,
among the black-eyed dreamers
his lungs empty,

but a seal's heart is full of love

which is perhaps what makes me
marvel at their watchful ways
and the perfect manner in which
they inhabit their bodies and dive
into the water which has carried them
to us and us to them.

PAUL PERRY

SWIMMING WITH SEALS

You can see she's still a dancer by her stretch
in reaching for a cup on a high shelf, how
she swims as one long sinew from fingertip
to pointed toe; an even stroke past the breakers.

We jump. The cold is a slap that leaves me
clutching at air. It doesn't even faze her.
We're at the bare edge of cliffs that rear up
so high overhead we arch onto our backs
to get their measure.

We can see past Dalkey Island to Portmarnock,
past Greystones' ruined harbour to Wicklow Head,
and two tyre-backed seals arise from nowhere,
heads cocked with questions. I tread water;

she goes out with them farther than I dare,
out to where the current sweeps hard left
towards Dublin Bay and the stream of it
catches the light, the nap of its surface
an oily river through the water.

She works the lines of her body, dives as they dive
and rise. They bob like needles embroidering
as they go below. They are alien
and fluent in the heaving sea.
Their motion translates as a kind of joy.

They always seem to be playing
even in the serious work of survival. Her brown back
weaves with the seals. She laughs
and in the yawn of sea and air it echoes.
The shock of the water snatches my breath.
And this steals whatever breath I had left.

ERIN FORNOFF

THE SEA LION

In the eyes of an old sea lion
which has buried itself in sand high up a beach,
to be left alone to die,
you meet your own reflection.

Does it see how nothing ends or begins,
does it see how empty the beach becomes
when the birds lift and the wind drops
and the light presses down? Does it see

the beach where it was born, each wave?
Do the unjoined rib and broken shell
scattered over the sand make it feel
something must hold everything together,

or does it, at the end, feel nothing,
no desire to remain, none to leave?
Does it see its life now as a rock
to which it knows it can't return,

is the wind all it feels, are wind and rock
about to become what they were before
these eyes were? These eyes into which
sand has already begun to drift.

MARK ROPER

LAMBS

On an evening that showed me once
how the end of August comes to sadden us,
I gathered up the fallen cones
in the corner of the yard,
in the shadow of the willow.
Then I walked as far as the thistle-field,
the stream without a ripple.
Along the track of indentations in the grass
to the place where cattle came to drink
from their reflections, and I to think.
I had questions to ask and all the answers
shook the branches of the trees,

made the hinges creak
on that old gate that locked us out, locked us in.
In the slaughterhouse lambs
were waiting, knives prepared
for the village butcher whose *coup de grace*
took half a minute. I remember him still,
slightly stooped, red-faced grin,
his apron like a pelt around him.
His black Wellingtons ankle-deep in entrails.

GERARD SMYTH

'WHO PRAYS ...'

Who prays at the graves
of the unbaptised children?
A sheep on its knees.

FRANCIS HARVEY (1925 – 2014)

THE SPIDER

The spider inhabits
the last unlit corners
a few hurried steps from turmoil.

It puts out one foot to test the waters
and you see a shadow glide
over the wall, just there, an inch above the skirting –

like a black vanishing point –
and disappear into the funereal
darkness behind the fridge,

for dark is its element and sinister us
its work, its *marche funèbre*
along the rope drawn

from its own heart
all the way to the abyss.
The spider has been there and back often

waving Its eight legs to an inaudible
inner music and in the place of nothing
behold – a dusty grey star

loose ends hooked over the mildewed
branches of a rosebush in October
or straying towards the North

shaky as a compass needle. If
the spider performs feats of hour-long
motionless cliff-hanging or bridging the void

with silk, it's as nothing
compared to its love of geometry. It gives not an inch
on radius even if carried too far

by its hunger for order
which suspends it between two rafters
at the exact ratio of 4:2.

Having seen enough of the world
it weaves nooses for its prey, lace traps, chiffon
shrouds spread all over the box hedge.

In the end it climbs into its dark nest
folds its symmetrical legs
and dies the lightest death.

EVA BOURKE

STARLINGS

I watched them from the window in our new estate –
swarming on the aerials and chimney pots,
the block of garages, the asphalt roof with the horse's head,
the broken plastic hoops, the tyre-tubes and plates.

From the smuts and clouds they showered down,
stabbing at our little patch of lawn
as yet more gathered on the sills and fence-posts,
sending out songs that mimicked ringing phones,

sirens, even failed ignitions on the road.
Speckled. Iridescent. They hunched in hundreds
on clotheslines, mowers, handlebars,
the iron bins and concrete bunkers of the yard.

And so this morning in the Dublin suburbs,
on a shortcut through a big estate,
telephone lines hung with trainers like coats of arms
on the gates of a fallen pile, I felt at home

around the pebbledash and worn-out lawns,
the yellow weeds, the painted ugly words.
The old heart's dial twitching once again.
The wintry electronica of birds.

JOHN KELLY

'WAVES THEMSELVES ...'

Waves themselves, their wings
flashing silver when they turn
as one – the starlings.

PAT BORAN

STORKS

They come in over the water like smoke,
long horizontals of vague crayon,
a shifting sentence whose sense and shape
is subject to constant correction.

From their rickety homes high on poles,
from villages all over the place
they've been lifted and added to themselves
and spiralled high into sky above sea.

Now they are one bird, one bird made
of hundreds of birds, one great drift
which would not seem to move a muscle
but alters all the while its every angle.

Across to this peninsula they shift and spread
and the bird made of all the birds
fills the air, rises and falls, a mix of sticks,
a fluent roof, a scattered floating thatch,

and a wing made out of many birds
(though never out of the same birds)
is opened out and stretched towards the ground.
There is something here they need to ascertain

and when you happen to glance out over the sea
the bird made of all birds, though right here,
is also spread out far into the distance,
drawn as if by an easy breath west.

MARK ROPER

SWALLOW

Sprays of red haw tell her it's time
to go, and she's springing from thorn,
feathered back brindled with sprigs
of damp straw, soft throat soaring free
of snagging bramble, winging south
over blackberry and furze. She has met
with nothing here but rain, the kind
of rain that flushes mountain ash
and chestnut from clogged earth.
Roadside hedgerows bow as she glides,
fuchsia lanterns flop to damp ground.
Soon she will be darting over miles
of dust track, past ghost shack and scrub,
glancing off rock cacti that do not sink roots
but run feelers lightly over dunes, cup rain
as it slides through spines.

MARY NOONAN

SWALLOWS

They hurl themselves above an acre of lawn
overlooking a tree-fringed lake. A paradise
of insects inspires them. They've lobbed
their fragile bodies over African swamp,
savannah, Saharan vastness, funnelled
into Europe through the Strait of Gibraltar
and flung themselves across to Ireland for this
aerial plankton. They're quick and agile

as their tiny prey: same darts, direction
changes, that give fly-swatting its tension.
They make it a gambol, their frenzied
metabolism fuelled by the flesh of thousands.
They dip, dive, swoop, loop, swarm
together, reel away, flatten out over
the blades, float up, circle and climb, then
peel off with a flash of sailor-white belly.
Every twist is a gauze of flickering wing;
each smooth-shouldered downstroke a surge
of orbital power, almost gravity-free
in a dart-like form that skims into long
shallow undulations. In sun, they iridesce
with indigo; in shade, they're swart as plum.
Blurred with speed, the fused pellet of head
and torso bisects a sickle of wing; only
time slows them enough to catch the tail's
lovely fork, the studs of white decorating
the membrane of its fan. They shark the air,
a dark unruly shoal, voices zipping staccato,
or, now, an unruly chirrip. Grown youngsters
buzz their parents across the grass
and they all rise, chittering, in a vertical dance,
its pinnacle an agape of bill, an insectivorous
kiss. Then they slide down the tent of air
and swerve off. Together, wings and tail
make a double pair, seen when they swing
their rumps forward, give a butterfly-flutter
to slow, to stall, to half-hover over some coarse
flower, transmuting their silhouette
to that Gabriel descended.

MARY MONTAGUE

FÁINLEOGA

Bhuail na bioráin binneas ceoil ón gciúnas,
greimeanna ag tuirlingt amhail fáinleoga
i scuaine ar sreang ag fáinne an lae,
iad ag faire ar shnáithín olla á shníomh
ina ghúinín cróchbhuí, gan lúb ar lár,

déanta di siúd
a d'fhan, is
a d'imigh léi
i bhfaiteadh na súl.

Sínte spréite i m'aonar
i bhfuacht an ospidéil,
cuimlím míne, gile
an ghúna le leathleiceann liom.
Scaoilim leis an tsnaidhm,
ligim le

                                      lúb

                        ar

               lúb

snáithe silte
fáinleoga ag titim as radharc
le luí na gréine.

Fásann an liathróid olla
i mo lámh: lúbtha, liath, lán.

DOIREANN NÍ GHRÍOFA

SWALLOWS

The knitting needles drew song from silence,
little stitches following each another
as dawn swallows gather on a wire,
peering at a skirt of yellow wool
that grew bright as a bruise, becoming

a dress
for a girl who came
and left
too soon.

Stretched in a narrow bed,
I lie in a corridor, alone. Cold,
I hold the small dress to my cheek
a moment, then unbind the knot,
and release

                                      stitch
                         after
                stitch

each unpicked, as swallows vanish
at dusk to some unfathomable land,
far from us.

I hold this soft unravelment as it grows,
and O, it grows, this un-wound wool. It grows. Dull. Full.

DOIREANN NÍ GHRÍOFA

SWAN HOUSE *(AN EXCERPT)*

And what were we to make of that swan
which came crashing through the mist, low
over the house like a lost glory,

so sudden it was gone before it came,
re-assumed into mist, its light
only seeming to reach us then, as if

we only saw it when we breathed the word *Swan*,
as if all recognition were farewell.

MARK ROPER

MADMAN. TWILIGHT.
PORTOBELLO BRIDGE

He rests.
He's had a busy afternoon.
Sixteen swans to say hello to.
And the man in the moon.

TOM MATHEWS

SWIFTS

I can't believe they don't know what they're doing
that delight is unknown to them as they gather
preparing for the long and terrible journey.
It can't merely be all programme, hard-wire, protein,
plasma, synapse, cellular. They are too expert
at elevation and elation, those twin joys.
The other day I walked down a street
of small grey houses in my neighbourhood
and saw them take off and settle around a pole
from which five parallel wires were strung
to other poles, from those onto the eaves. There was
such excitement in the air, flutter
and twitter of a great activity, swing-up, dip
and vibrato of landing on the shakiest of landing strips,
their arrow-tailed dark bodies arranged on the
electric wires like quavers on a large grey sheet of music.
I picked out and sang the melody they'd composed
in thirds and fifths, two Ds, three Gs, two Bs, and two
    more Ds,
then the whole gamut upped and modulated in one lift-off
to the top line F and with extravagant slurs
and glissandi flocked onto a nearby gutter.
A neighbour opening her door behind me said
they're gathering to say goodbye and will soon be away.
I sang the swifts' song to her then as best I could
but never mastered the mordents of farewell
as they slipped past us and beyond.

EVA BOURKE

PARADOXES

Caged in a doorway between garden and conservatory
the Peachfaced Love Bird trills a Niagara.
The family replenish seed and water.

Emily dead-heads red anemones,
allows sun to quiver along the backs
of her slender hands; listens intently

to the Song Thrush's warble. In an eye-blink
it's gone, rudder guiding through blue sky
to land on a school's nervy weathervane.

A tortoiseshell, tissue from bone of the sun,
alights on Emily's crinoline, as if stitched, integral
to the dress. Without warning, it's swallowed by hibiscus.

Her bedroom is spare as a Puritan pew.
Before writing she feels the cold breath
of her grandfather over her shoulder,

muddied spade in hand. She shrugs
him off, goes on tilling white acres;
pen-furrows natural as the bird's throaty song.

RAY GIVANS

MISTLE THRUSH (FROM 'SUBURB')

The sycamore is weeping leaves of fire;
a maple stands in its own flaming lake;

shy birches isolate in yellow puddles.
You'd half expect these young trees to kick

their fallen skirts away. Bride? Bullfighter?
Dervish dancer rapt in a swirling cape?
When I went out an hour ago to muddle
through the leafdrift at my door, a flock

of mistle thrush descended – a deputation
from the wingéd world with urgent and with fatal news:
Dying is simple. You breathe in, you breathe out, you
    breathe in,
you breathe out and you don't breathe in again.
They acted like this was cause for celebration
– the first minor chord of my winter blues.

PAULA MEEHAN

LONGTAILED TITS

A soft settling, sift of whisper, chink
and chitter and you're in the middle

of urgent conversation, six or seven
or eight or nine or ten of them talking

all at once *listen to me no you listen to me*
no you listen no you a carry-on hidden

in trees a speaking of leaves is it
a house of sound a second skin

a desperate *I'm here but where are you,*
birds vague in colour, light as dust,

so small they'd soon get lost in silence,
slip through cracks in the day, it's all

around you now tiny travelling circus
you're hanging on every word afraid

you'll miss something then it's gone
and you're hurrying after you're calling

wait, I didn't catch that, what did you say,
sorry, don't mean to be rude, it was just that

MARK ROPER

TOAD

Warted as maybe a witch is, or 'ugly and venomous'
according to the exiled Duke in *As You Like It*,
or a metaphor for the cold, squatting thing felt to exist,
Philip Larkin's poem asserts, both outside
and inside a life – you yet carry your robust self,
your cladding of lichened colours, back far
before us, to the epoch of dinosaurs. Snibs of rock,
effervesces of air trapped in ancient ice, fossils
and other artefacts – these help unlock primal secrets.
But if I suggest I can discern behind your eyes
sights your ancestors may well have seen –
of horrendous *Hatzegopteryx*, for example, crouched

under tarpaulin of leathery wing-webbing,
or juddering its head as it swallows a smaller animal;
or if in my enthusiasm I credit you contain,
buried deep inside your brain, no gemstone or antidote
to poison, but a residual spectre of terror,
the comet blast of impact winter that all but finished
everything – well, this skew-whiff song I offer
cherishes, still, your muddling through, your survival.

PATRICK DEELEY

VULTURE

A sheepman in the Mournes observed it first
gorging on the entrails of a still-born
lamb; next it was disturbed plucking the heart
from an aborted human foetus unborn

for better things elsewhere and on the third
day poachers stoned it from the corpse of an
informer they found gagged with a dragon's turd
and testicles. But it grew weary on
such rich fare, scavenging the abattoirs
of hate until, enormous, gross, and fat
with the viscera of the dove and rat,

sated yet home-sick for the heat and flies,
it bore South again, smelling a sweeter war
where God died long ago of tribal lies.

FRANCIS HARVEY (1925 – 2014)

SEPTEMBER

Wasps, then rain. Below, streets clear
to a silent siren. Some citizens scatter,
others stand looking upwards.

Wasps nestle into the neck
of abandoned sugar canisters, the wood
of balconies sways.

In parks the remnants of summer
still – dug-up earth, a brittle mound
of clay, some small animal's refuge.

The leaves here are beginning to fall.
Sun-bleached, they swirl like shadows
in the *Föhn*, like shadows adjusting.

LEEANNE QUINN

EACH DAY THE QUEEN WASP CAME

at first I thought it always the same creature –
September turning to October and her regular flight
in through any open window – but then two came. Three.

October yielded to November and still they came
buzzing their insistent daily drone, demanding
their abundance was a portent I should read.

Lone sovereigns, I feared everything about them:
their sickening clash of black and yellow armour,
all that latent, formidable power, as though

when they flew into my rooms, I'd drawn a dark card,
Death or The Tower reversed and they heralded
transformation through some unavoidable sting.

Late autumn, last leaves on the chestnut,
I faced my fears, researched wasps, tracing
my fortune between the lines of science. *Come,*

they whispered, *it is time to over-winter. Be tenacious.*
Live by the lamp of your own scent, Queen wasp, complete.
Not ready for any voice to tell me I was built

for such aloneness, I almost gave up divination –
but then I read how few queens survive,
that if they live, they only live a year

and I knew the wasps didn't care
about my aloneness or whatever I might
or might not achieve, they were saying,

Do this for me: love with abandon the physical world.

GRACE WELLS

THE SONG OF THE WHALE

And the whale beached
In Lislarry. And they brought the JCB
And buried it. All thirty foot of it.
They said it was black,
Shining skin from the sea.
Grey blue, some argued
All thirty foot of it.
And the whale men came,
They came all the way from Cork,
For that is where the whale men
And the dolphin men hang out,
And they made their notes
And ecological plans and took
Blood samples and measured the tide
So that the whale now lies
Under the limestone reaches,
Proud steps to the summer storm,
Turquoise and shimmering,
Great sea mammal, partner of song.

LELAND BARDWELL (1922 – 2016)

THE LAST WOLF IN IRELAND

Before, dark star of eagle; herds of elk
Lumbering through forests, gloom of oak

Hewn since by the acre, shipped to become
The ribs of abbeys and cathedrals, hum

Of parliament – their fists thumping the benches
Made from wood we'd marked as ours, stain of piss,

As they proclaimed the laws that soon would find us
Gasping in the ditches. Only the legends

Left behind: the stolen infant, suckled
Amongst cubs; the woolskin covering each pelt

While we moved stealthy through the dozing flock.
No mercy when we needed to attack;

An airy rush, fur tumbling to claw,
Muscle and sinew, our mouths rusting with gore.

Now I paw the undergrowth for carrion, snuffling
Beneath bushes, and watch the soldiers clanking

Into villages. Land being sheared and trimmed;
The new estates. Fire scented on the wind:

A country turned out, turning on its own as
Bounty hunters oil their muskets. Shadows

Over moonlit fields, the locals' silvered faces
Pointing out our sleeping young, the hidden places

They'll name after us when I am also gone
To earth among wing-feathers, antler bone,

The bog dreamtime; in black sod sunk below
Where no shone steel will ever fence or plough.

JOHN O'DONNELL

BLACK WOLF

Real this time. Not
myth-broil, story-weave,
to thicken the pearl of imagination,
make the personal fabulous,
survivable; but bought
with common currencies –
work, time, technology –
distilled to a series of steps:
go to Minnesota; get in a Cessna;
follow the clicks of a radio-collar.

Still, the dark wolf of the mind
is less a surprise
than the wolf of the North Woods.

As the aircraft roars to search height,
terrain becomes a mange of shadow
and snow, thick pelt of spruce, fir,
stippling to bristles of aspen and birch
that bald to the clean-edged blankness
of snow-smothered frozen lake.
Under the plane's wings, flat

antlers of antennae listen for signals
from the Moose Lake pack.

This high, trails are broken capillaries
fretting the lakes' white faces: furrows,
skims, that mark how an animal ploughed
or leaped through chest-deep snow.
Once, a tiny silhouette: a white-tailed deer
like a decoration stencilled on seasonal icing.

Approaching the recognised territory of known
wolves, but miles from where telemetry
will translate sound into sight, the voice
of the pilot, a casual shout, *oh there's one*,
and the plane banks giddyingly
to slide the wolf into view.

Call it coincidence, call it
what you will. The mind closes,
hisses, that what it conjured
and what's out there
don't converge like this;

the world is not made
to give signs and wonders;
has its own laws, its own
necessary evolvings.

It is not there to provide personal comfort.

And then it does.

So you made it to wolf country.

You were promised a sighting.
Now there's your black wolf,
uncollared, on an open plain
of lake. Your retinas burn
as sun switches on the snow.
This is not the same. The animal
is slightly ludicrous as it leaps, furious,
rump swivelling in a push for altitude,
head agitated to see off this infernal
noisy bird that holds you in its bowels.

Which is the true wolf? The one
you made up? Or this large wild dog
dancing in vigorous useless challenge?

The pilot pulls away, flies on to the named
numbered tracked pack we've come to see.
The wolves are bedded, curled like walnuts.

On the sickening return, your eyes cast
for where a snow-bruise breaks a long
thread between the cover of trees;

where the song of the mind was greeted
by the dark flesh of the world.

MARY MONTAGUE

WOODPECKER

You come home and tell me you've seen,
for the first time, a woodpecker,
feeding at the coconut shell
hung in your brother-in-law's tree.

What kind was it I want to know.
There are 3 kinds, black, green, spotted.
One laughs, it's known as a yaffle.
There aren't any in Ireland.

You can't remember its colour.
It flew slowly down to the tree,
edged its way out towards the shell,
began to eat, you can see it now

and you shape it in the air for me,
one hand carefully cupping
the weight of what it meant,
you hold it there for me as if

I'd never broken anything
you'd ever given me and it starts
to cross the space between us
and I do not know what to say.

MARK ROPER

WOODWORM

Riddle of pores, anti-braille,
unreadable merely
as symptom or outcome,

and if not world in itself
then a way of the world,
each larval harrowing

a patient, silent
invisible graft
that works for years

beneath the thinnest
of veneers before the sudden
emergence. How deep,

you ask, do they go,
these careful burrows? Well,
How long have you got?

As your capillaries,
unravelled, might reach
to the moon and back,

so the galleries inside
this single chest
laid end to end

could girdle the earth,
the four-square box so hollowed
a single glance could overturn it.

CONOR CARVILLE

RED WRIGGLERS

Benevolent in a spadeful
of soil, if spared the beak
they will burrow down to earth,

disappear into the underworld,
a journey through the Neolithic
handbag, the dead red lips

kissing the new life,
wriggling back into the black
where once it all began.

MATTHEW GEDEN

WORM SONG

Articulated
servant of the plain truth
seldom stated,

part link, part chain,
serpent echo
in the slow lane

though sawn in half
on your journey
to the heart

of darkest matter. O lonely
shunting of the earth song
too low to sing; O hole

in the ring; O dull
but faithful sexton
of hallowed ground,

of growth and change,
pushing ahead
(again, and still again)

to where the sun
can never enter
though the rain seeps in –

O mindless worker,
blind muck-raker,
self-buried miner,

in your endless night
unmake all this, we pray,
to make it all alright.

PAT BORAN

WREN

The whirr of trapped panicky wings, a small
Thump, then silence. When I found you lying
In a double-glazed stupor near the window
And held you in my cupped hands, little king

Of all birds I thought you'd never live
Until Stephen's Day to be caught in the furze.
To cover you and keep you warm was just
A kindness towards your quivering frailty.

So when, again unseen, you pushed aside
Your winding-sheet and whirred straight out
The open door, it was like found money
To hurry to the window and to see you.

Tail cocked, strutting your tiny stuff
In and out of crevices in a wall,
Exploring pockets of light and air
Between the weight and darkness of the stones.

And when you climbed the ladder of seed-pods
To sway and sing in the ruffling wind,
My heart sang too, as if suddenly lifted
To majestic heights on an eagle's back.

PADDY BUSHE

CREDITS AND ACKNOWLEDGEMENTS

The poems in this volume are drawn from the following books available from The Dedalus Press. Thanks to the poets and copyright holders for their permission to include them herein. To save space here, full information on all titles as well as biographical details of the contributing poets may be found at *www.dedaluspress.com*.

LELAND BARDWELL from *Them's Your Mammy's Pills and other poems (2015)*; PAT BORAN from *New and Selected Poems* (2007), *The Next Life* (2012), *Waveforms: Bull Island Haiku* (Orange Crate Books, 2015) and *Then Again* (2019); EVA BOURKE from *Spring in Henry Street* (1996), *Travels with Gandolpho* (2000), *piano* (2011) and *Seeing Yellow* (2018); PADDY BUSHE from *To Ring in Silence: New and Selected Poems* (2008), *On A Turning Wing* (2016) and *Second Sight* (2020); CONOR CARVILLE from *Harm's Way* (2013); INGER CHRISTENSEN from *Butterfly Valley*, trans. Susanna Nied (2012); MARIE COVENEY from *Measuring: Dedalus New Writers 1* (2012); ENDA COYLE-GREENE from *Snow Negatives (2007)* and *Map of the Last (2013)*; CATHERINE ANN CULLEN from *The Other Now* (2016); PÁDRAIG J DALY from *Clinging to the Myth (2007)* and *Afterlife (2010)*; PATRICK DEELEY from *Groundswell: New and Selected Poems* (2013) and *The End of the World* (2019); THEO DORGAN from *Orpheus (2018)*; KATHERINE DUFFY from *Sorrow's Egg (2011)*; ERIN FORNOFF *from Hymn to the Reckless* (2017); MATTHEW GEDEN from *The Place Inside* (2012); RAY GIVANS from *Tolstoy in Love* (2009); FRANCIS HARVEY from *Collected Poems* (2007) and *Donegal Haiku* (2013); ELEANOR HOOKER from *A Tug of Blue* (2016); PATRICK KEHOE from *The Cask of*

Moonlight (2014); JOHN KELLY from *Notions* (2018); CATHERINE PHIL MacCARTHY from *The Invisible Threshold* (2012) and *Daughters of the House* (2019); TOM MATHEWS from *The Owl and the Pussycat and Other Poems* (2009) and *No Return Game* (2013); PHILIP McDONAGH from *The Song the Oriole Sang* (2010); IGGY McGOVERN from *Safe House* (2010); PAULA MEEHAN from *Geomantic* (2016) and *As If By Magic: Selected Poems* (forthcoming, 2020); MARY MONTAGUE from *Tribe* (2008); AIDAN MURPHY from *The Wrong Side of Town* (2015); GERRY MURPHY from *End of Part One: New and Selected Poems* (2006) and *My Flirtation with International Socialism* (2010); DOIREANN Ní GHRÍOFA from *Lies* (2018); MARY NOONAN from *The Fado House* (2012); PEGGY O'BRIEN from *Frog Spotting* (2009); JOHN O'DONNELL from *Sunlight: New and Selected Poems* (2018); MARY O'DONOGHUE from *Among These Winters* (2007); PAUL PERRY from *The Orchard Keeper* (2006); LEEANNE QUINN from *Some Lives* (forthcoming, 2020); GER REIDY from *Drifting Under the Moon* (2010); MARK ROPER from *Even So: New and Selected Poems* (2008) and *Bindweed* (2017); GERARD SMYTH from *The Fullness of Time: New and Selected Poems* (2010); ROSS THOMPSON from *Threading the Light* (2019); RICHARD TILLINGHAST from *Selected Poems* (2009); JESSICA TRAYNOR from *Liffey Swim* (2014) and *The Quick* (2018); GRACE WELLS from *When God Has Been Called Away to Greater Things* (2010) and *Fur* (2015); JOSEPH WOODS from *Cargo* (2010) and *Ocean Letters* (2011); MACDARA WOODS from *Collected Poems* (2012); and ENDA WYLEY from *Poems for Breakfast* (2004), *Borrowed Space: New and Selected Poems* (2014) and *The Painter on his Bike* (2019).

DEDALUS PRESS

Named for James Joyce's literary alter ego,
Dedalus Press is one of Ireland's longest running
and best-known literary imprints, dedicated to
contemporary Irish poetry, and to poetry
from around the world in English translation.

For more information, or to purchase copies
of this or other Dedalus Press titles,
please visit us at *www.dedaluspress.com.*

*"One of the most outward-looking
poetry presses in Ireland and the UK"*
—UNESCO.org

Poetry Matters:
Spread the Word